American Spirit

Student Workbook | Part 1

A Demme Learning Publication

American Spirit Student Workbook, Parts 1 and 2
©2014 Spelling You See
©2013 Karen J. Holinga, PhD
Published and distributed by Demme Learning

All rights reserved. No part of this book may be reproduced, stored in a retrieval system, or transmitted in any form by any means—electronic, mechanical, photocopying, recording, or otherwise—without prior written permission from Demme Learning.

spellingyousee.com

1-888-854-6284 or +1 717-283-1448 | demmelearning.com
Lancaster, Pennsylvania USA

ISBN 978-1-60826-615-9 (American Spirit Student Workbook)
ISBN 978-1-60826-616-6 (Part 1)

Revision Code 1118-F

Printed in the United States of America by CJK Group
10 9 8 7 6 5 4 3 2 1

For information regarding CPSIA on this printed material call: 1-888-854-6284 and provide reference #1118-03282024

To the Instructor

This innovative program is designed to help your student become a confident and successful speller while spending only a few minutes each day on spelling practice. The program is not difficult, but it is different. Your *Instructor's Handbook* is essential in order to teach this program effectively.

Before you begin, take time to read **Getting Started** in the *Handbook*, as well as the detailed directions for the first few lessons. As you move through the various activities, you will also want to read more details about each one in the **Weekly Activity Guide**. There is an answer key in the back of the *Handbook* that shows exactly how each passage in the student book should be marked.

For a more in-depth understanding of the program, read the sections about the philosophy and the developmental stages of spelling. You will also find the answers to **Frequently Asked Questions** helpful.

1A Section 1: Vowel Chunks

1. Read the story to your student.
2. Read it together slowly. Encourage your student to look carefully at each word.
3. Vowel chunks are a combination of vowels that usually make one sound. Help your student find and mark all the **vowel chunks** in yellow.

Colonial children liked having fun as much as you do. Of course, they didn't have video games or movies. They found many other ways to have a good time. They played tag, hopscotch, and hide and seek. They rolled hoops, shot marbles, and beat drums. They played with dolls and tea sets. A group could play rounders, a game something like baseball. Colonial children worked hard. They also found many ways to play.

Vowel Chunks

aa	ae	ai	ao	au	aw	ay
ea	ee	ei	eo	ew	ey	eau
ia	ie	ii	io	iu		
oa	oe	oi	oo	ou	ow	oy
ua	ue	ui	uo	uy		

American Spirit Student

Section 2: Copywork

Copy the story and mark the vowel chunks that you marked in Section 1.

Colonial children liked having fun
C

as much as you do. Of course,
a

they didn't have video games or
t

movies. They found many other
m

ways to have a good time. They
w

played tag, hopscotch, and hide
p

and seek. They rolled hoops, shot
a

marbles, and beat drums. They
m

played with dolls and tea sets.
p

1B Section 1: Vowel Chunks

1. Read the story to your student.
2. Read it together slowly. Encourage your student to look carefully at each word.
3. Work with your student to find all the **vowel chunks** and mark them in yellow.

Colonial children liked having fun as much as you do. Of course, they didn't have video games or movies. They found many other ways to have a good time. They played tag, hopscotch, and hide and seek. They rolled hoops, shot marbles, and beat drums. They played with dolls and tea sets. A group could play rounders, a game something like baseball. Colonial children worked hard. They also found many ways to play.

Vowel Chunks

aa	ae	ai	ao	au	aw	ay
ea	ee	ei	eo	ew	ey	eau
ia	ie	ii	io	iu		
oa	oe	oi	oo	ou	ow	oy
ua	ue	ui	uo	uy		

Section 2: Copywork

Copy and "chunk" the story. Look at the opposite page if you need help.

They played tag, hopscotch, and
T
hide and seek. They rolled hoops,
h
shot marbles, and beat drums.
s
They played with dolls and tea
T
sets. A group could play rounders,
s
a game something like baseball.
a
Colonial children worked hard.
C
They also found many ways
T
to play.
t

American Spirit Student **1B**

1C Section 1: Vowel Chunks

1. Read the story to your student.
2. Read it together slowly. Encourage your student to look carefully at each word.
3. Together, find all the **vowel chunks** in the passage and mark them in yellow.

Colonial children liked having fun as much as you do. Of course, they didn't have video games or movies. They found many other ways to have a good time. They played tag, hopscotch, and hide and seek. They rolled hoops, shot marbles, and beat drums. They played with dolls and tea sets. A group could play rounders, a game something like baseball. Colonial children worked hard. They also found many ways to play.

Vowel Chunks

aa	ae	ai	ao	au	aw	ay
ea	ee	ei	eo	ew	ey	eau
ia	ie	ii	io	iu		
oa	oe	oi	oo	ou	ow	oy
ua	ue	ui	uo	uy		

American Spirit Student

Section 2: Copywork

Copy and chunk the story. Look at the opposite page if you need help.

Colonial children liked having fun

C

as much as you do. Of course,

a

they didn't have video games or

t

movies. They found many other

m

ways to have a good time. They

w

played tag, hopscotch, and hide

p

and seek. They rolled hoops, shot

a

marbles, and beat drums. They

m

played with dolls and tea sets.

p

1D

Section 1: Vowel Chunks

1. Read the story to your student.

2. Read it together slowly. Encourage your student to look carefully at each word.

3. Together, find all the <u>vowel chunks</u> in the passage and mark them in yellow.

4. Before doing the dictation, be sure to watch the video demonstrating how to do it. All the passages in this workbook are also in the *Instructor's Handbook* under Resources. When dictating the passage, you may want to cover this page with a piece of paper and read the story from the *Handbook*.

Colonial children liked having fun as much as you do. Of course, they didn't have video games or movies. They found many other ways to have a good time. They played tag, hopscotch, and hide and seek. They rolled hoops, shot marbles, and beat drums. They played with dolls and tea sets. A group could play rounders, a game something like baseball. Colonial children worked hard. They also found many ways to play.

Vowel Chunks

aa	ae	ai	ao	au	aw	ay
ea	ee	ei	eo	ew	ey	eau
ia	ie	ii	io	iu		
oa	oe	oi	oo	ou	ow	oy
ua	ue	ui	uo	uy		

Section 2: First Dictation

Write this week's story from dictation. Take your time and ask for help if you need it.

Colonial

I spelled _____ words correctly.

1E Section 1: Vowel Chunks

1. Read the story to your student.
2. Read it together slowly. Encourage your student to look carefully at each word.
3. Together, find all the **vowel chunks** in the passage and mark them in yellow.

Colonial children liked having fun as much as you do. Of course, they didn't have video games or movies. They found many other ways to have a good time. They played tag, hopscotch, and hide and seek. They rolled hoops, shot marbles, and beat drums. They played with dolls and tea sets. A group could play rounders, a game something like baseball. Colonial children worked hard. They also found many ways to play.

Vowel Chunks

aa	ae	ai	ao	au	aw	ay
ea	ee	ei	eo	ew	ey	eau
ia	ie	ii	io	iu		
oa	oe	oi	oo	ou	ow	oy
ua	ue	ui	uo	uy		

Section 2: Second Dictation

See if you can write this week's story from dictation without asking for help.

American Spirit Student 1E   **I spelled _____ words correctly.**

2A Section 1: Vowel Chunks

1. Read the story to your student.
2. Read it together slowly. Encourage your student to look carefully at each word.
3. Together, find all the <u>vowel chunks</u> in the passage and mark them in yellow.

A frail little slave girl was sold to the Wheatley family. They named her Phillis after the slave ship that had brought her to Boston. Slaves were not allowed to go to school. The Wheatleys taught Phillis to read and write. She learned very quickly. As a teenager, Phillis Wheatley began writing poems. She was the first African American poet to have her poems printed.

Vowel Chunks

aa	ae	ai	ao	au	aw	ay
ea	ee	ei	eo	ew	ey	eau
ia	ie	ii	io	iu		
oa	oe	oi	oo	ou	ow	oy
ua	ue	ui	uo	uy		

American Spirit Student

Section 2: Copywork

Copy and chunk the story. Look at the opposite page if you need help.

A frail little slave girl was sold
A
to the Wheatley family. They
t
named her Phillis after the slave
n
ship that had brought her to
s
Boston. Slaves were not allowed
B
to go to school. The Wheatleys
t
taught Phillis to read and write.
t
She learned very quickly.
S

2B
Section 1: Vowel Chunks

1. Read the story to your student.
2. Read it together slowly. Encourage your student to look carefully at each word.
3. Together, find all the **vowel chunks** in the passage and mark them in yellow.

A frail little slave girl was sold to the Wheatley family. They named her Phillis after the slave ship that had brought her to Boston. Slaves were not allowed to go to school. The Wheatleys taught Phillis to read and write. She learned very quickly. As a teenager, Phillis Wheatley began writing poems. She was the first African American poet to have her poems printed.

Vowel Chunks

aa ae ai ao au aw ay

ea ee ei eo ew ey eau

ia ie ii io iu

oa oe oi oo ou ow oy

ua ue ui uo uy

American Spirit Student

Section 2: Copywork
Copy and chunk the story. Look at the opposite page if you need help.

Slaves were not allowed to
S

go to school. The Wheatleys
g

taught Phillis to read and write.
t

She learned very quickly. As a
S

teenager, Phillis Wheatley began
t

writing poems. She was the first
w

African American poet to have
A

her poems printed.
h

2C
Section 1: Vowel Chunks

1. Read the story to your student.
2. Read it together slowly. Encourage your student to look carefully at each word.
3. Together, find all the **vowel chunks** in the passage and mark them in yellow.

A frail little slave girl was sold to the Wheatley family. They named her Phillis after the slave ship that had brought her to Boston. Slaves were not allowed to go to school. The Wheatleys taught Phillis to read and write. She learned very quickly. As a teenager, Phillis Wheatley began writing poems. She was the first African American poet to have her poems printed.

Vowel Chunks

aa ae ai ao au aw ay
ea ee ei eo ew ey eau
ia ie ii io iu
oa oe oi oo ou ow oy
ua ue ui uo uy

American Spirit Student

Section 2: Copywork

Copy and chunk the story. Look at the opposite page if you need help.

A frail little slave girl was sold

A

to the Wheatley family. They

t

named her Phillis after the slave

n

ship that had brought her to

s

Boston. Slaves were not allowed

B

to go to school. The Wheatleys

t

taught Phillis to read and write.

t

She learned very quickly.

S

2D

Section 1: Vowel Chunks

1. Read the story to your student.
2. Read it together slowly. Encourage your student to look carefully at each word.
3. Together, find all the **vowel chunks** in the passage and mark them in yellow.

A frail little slave girl was sold to the Wheatley family. They named her Phillis after the slave ship that had brought her to Boston. Slaves were not allowed to go to school. The Wheatleys taught Phillis to read and write. She learned very quickly. As a teenager, Phillis Wheatley began writing poems. She was the first African American poet to have her poems printed.

Vowel Chunks

aa ae ai ao au aw ay

ea ee ei eo ew ey eau

ia ie ii io iu

oa oe oi oo ou ow oy

ua ue ui uo uy

Section 2: First Dictation

Write this week's story from dictation. Take your time and ask for help if you need it.

A

2E
Section 1: Vowel Chunks

1. Read the story to your student.
2. Read it together slowly. Encourage your student to look carefully at each word.
3. Together, find all the **vowel chunks** in the passage and mark them in yellow.

A frail little slave girl was sold to the Wheatley family. They named her Phillis after the slave ship that had brought her to Boston. Slaves were not allowed to go to school. The Wheatleys taught Phillis to read and write. She learned very quickly. As a teenager, Phillis Wheatley began writing poems. She was the first African American poet to have her poems printed.

Vowel Chunks

aa	ae	ai	ao	au	aw	ay
ea	ee	ei	eo	ew	ey	eau
ia	ie	ii	io	iu		
oa	oe	oi	oo	ou	ow	oy
ua	ue	ui	uo	uy		

Section 2: Second Dictation

See if you can write this week's story from dictation without asking for help.

3A Section 1: Consonant Chunks

1. Read the story to your student.
2. Read it together slowly. Have the student look carefully at each word as you read.
3. Help your student look for and mark all the **consonant chunks** in blue.

Benjamin Franklin loved swimming. He wanted to swim even faster. He shaped two pieces of thin wood into ovals. He cut a hole in each for his thumb. He may have gotten the idea from amphibians like frogs that have webbed feet. Ben swam much faster with these wooden fins, but he stopped using them. They made his wrists tired. Franklin had many other great ideas!

Consonant Chunks

ch	gh	ph	sh	th	wh	
gn	kn	qu	wr	dg	ck	tch
bb	cc	dd	ff	gg	hh	kk	ll	mm
nn	pp	rr	ss	tt	ww	vv	zz

Section 2: Copywork
Copy and chunk the story. Look at the opposite page if you need help.

Benjamin Franklin loved

B

swimming. He wanted to swim

s

even faster. He shaped two

e

pieces of thin wood into ovals.

p

He cut a hole in each for

H

his thumb. He may have gotten

h

the idea from amphibians like

t

frogs that have webbed feet.

f

Ben swam much faster

B

American Spirit Student 3A

3B
Section 1: Consonant Chunks

1. Read the story to your student.
2. Read it together slowly. Have the student look carefully at each word as you read.
3. Help your student look for and mark all the **consonant chunks** in blue. Notice that a consonant chunk may have a different sound than the individual letters do.

Benjamin Franklin loved swimming. He wanted to swim even faster. He shaped two pieces of thin wood into ovals. He cut a hole in each for his thumb. He may have gotten the idea from amphibians like frogs that have webbed feet. Ben swam much faster with these wooden fins, but he stopped using them. They made his wrists tired. Franklin had many other great ideas!

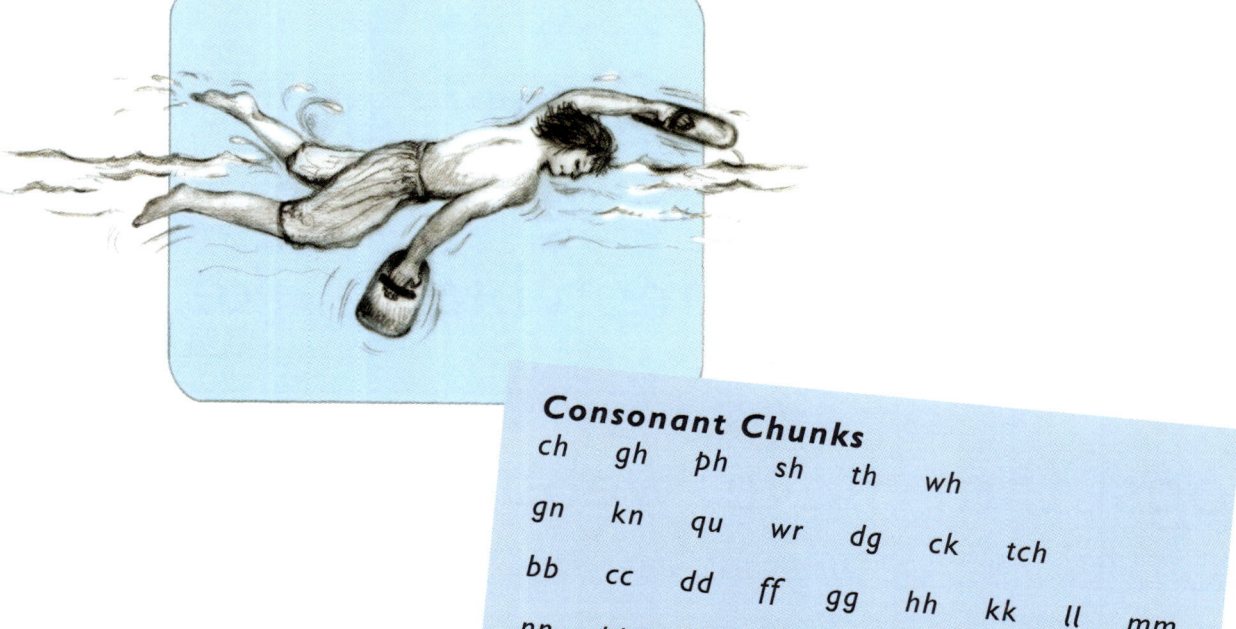

Consonant Chunks

ch	gh	ph	sh	th	wh		
gn	kn	qu	wr	dg	ck	tch	
bb	cc	dd	ff	gg	hh	kk	ll	mm
nn	pp	rr	ss	tt	ww	vv	zz

Section 2: Copywork

Copy and chunk the story. Look at the opposite page if you need help.

He cut a hole in each for

H

his thumb. He may have gotten

h

the idea from amphibians like

t

frogs that have webbed feet.

f

Ben swam much faster with

B

these wooden fins, but he

t

stopped using them. They made

s

his wrists tired. Franklin had

h

many other great ideas!

m

American Spirit Student 3B

3C Section 1: Consonant Chunks

1. Read the story to your student.
2. Read it together slowly. Have the student look carefully at each word as you read.
3. Help your student look for and mark all the **consonant chunks** in blue.

Benjamin Franklin loved swimming. He wanted to swim even faster. He shaped two pieces of thin wood into ovals. He cut a hole in each for his thumb. He may have gotten the idea from amphibians like frogs that have webbed feet. Ben swam much faster with these wooden fins, but he stopped using them. They made his wrists tired. Franklin had many other great ideas!

Consonant Chunks

ch	gh	ph	sh	th	wh		
gn	kn	qu	wr	dg	ck	tch	
bb	cc	dd	ff	gg	hh	kk	ll	mm
nn	pp	rr	ss	tt	ww	vv	zz

Section 2: Copywork

Copy and chunk the story. Look at the opposite page if you need help.

Benjamin Franklin loved

B

swimming. He wanted to swim

s

even faster. He shaped two

e

pieces of thin wood into ovals.

P

He cut a hole in each for

H

his thumb. He may have gotten

h

the idea from amphibians like

t

frogs that have webbed feet.

f

Ben swam much faster

B

3D

Section 1: Consonant Chunks

1. Read the story to your student.
2. Read it together slowly. Have the student look carefully at each word as you read.
3. Together, find all the **consonant chunks** in the passage and mark them in blue.

Benjamin Franklin loved swimming. He wanted to swim even faster. He shaped two pieces of thin wood into ovals. He cut a hole in each for his thumb. He may have gotten the idea from amphibians like frogs that have webbed feet. Ben swam much faster with these wooden fins, but he stopped using them. They made his wrists tired. Franklin had many other great ideas!

Consonant Chunks

ch	gh	ph	sh	th	wh	
gn	kn	qu	wr	dg	ck	tch
bb	cc	dd	ff	gg	hh	kk	ll	mm
nn	pp	rr	ss	tt	ww	vv	zz

Section 2: First Dictation

Write this week's story from dictation. Take your time and ask for help if you need it.

Benjamin

3E
Section 1: Consonant Chunks

1. Read the story to your student.
2. Read it together slowly. Have the student look carefully at each word as you read.
3. Together, find all the **consonant chunks** in the passage and mark them in blue.

Benjamin Franklin loved swimming. He wanted to swim even faster. He shaped two pieces of thin wood into ovals. He cut a hole in each for his thumb. He may have gotten the idea from amphibians like frogs that have webbed feet. Ben swam much faster with these wooden fins, but he stopped using them. They made his wrists tired. Franklin had many other great ideas!

Consonant Chunks

ch	gh	ph	sh	th	wh
gn	kn	qu	wr	dg	ck	tch
bb	cc	dd	ff	gg	hh	kk	ll	mm
nn	pp	rr	ss	tt	ww	vv	zz

Section 2: Second Dictation

See if you can write this week's story from dictation without asking for help.

Section 1: Consonant Chunks

1. Read the story to your student.
2. Read it together slowly. Have the student look carefully at each word as you read.
3. Help your student look for and mark all the <u>consonant chunks</u> in blue.

In colonial times, people used quill pens to write. A quill is the hollow shaft inside a feather. The tip of the feather is cut to form a point. Then the shaft is filled with ink. Learning to write with a quill pen takes time and practice. After every few words, the pen runs out of ink. Then you must refill it from an inkwell. The ballpoint pens we have today are much easier to use!

Consonant Chunks

ch	gh	ph	sh	th	wh
gn	kn	qu	wr	dg	ck	tch
bb	cc	dd	ff	gg	hh	kk	ll	mm
nn	pp	rr	ss	tt	ww	vv	zz

Section 2: Copywork

Copy and chunk the story. Look at the opposite page if you need help.

In colonial times, people used
I
quill pens to write. A quill is the
q
hollow shaft inside a feather.
h
The tip of the feather is cut to
T
form a point. Then the shaft is
f
filled with ink. Learning to write
f
with a quill pen takes time and
w
practice. After every few words,
p
the pen runs out of ink.
t

American Spirit Student 4A

4B
Section 1: Consonant Chunks

1. Read the story to your student.
2. Read it together slowly. Have the student look carefully at each word as you read.
3. Help your student look for and mark all the <u>consonant chunks</u> in blue.

In colonial times, people used quill pens to write. A quill is the hollow shaft inside a feather. The tip of the feather is cut to form a point. Then the shaft is filled with ink. Learning to write with a quill pen takes time and practice. After every few words, the pen runs out of ink. Then you must refill it from an inkwell. The ballpoint pens we have today are much easier to use!

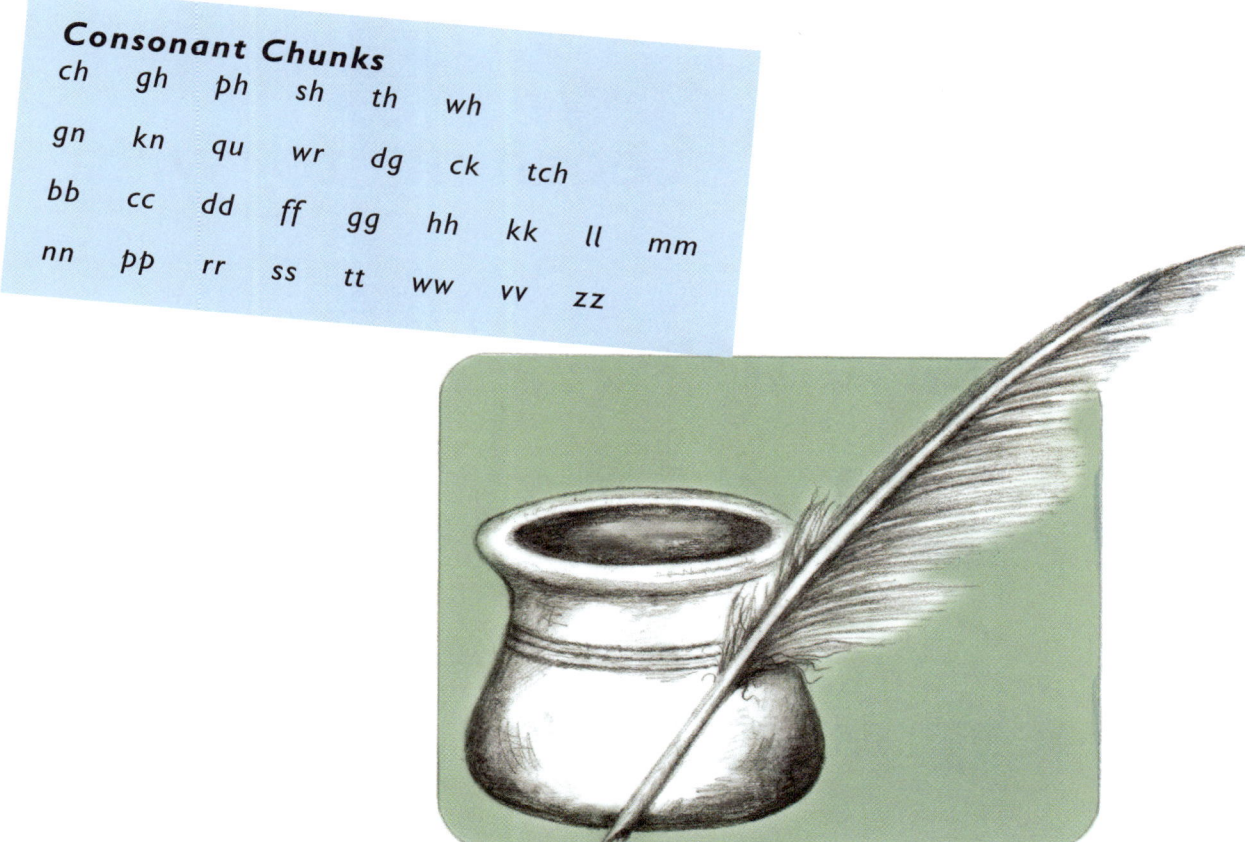

Consonant Chunks

ch	gh	ph	sh	th	wh		
gn	kn	qu	wr	dg	ck	tch	
bb	cc	dd	ff	gg	hh	kk	ll	mm
nn	pp	rr	ss	tt	ww	vv	zz

Section 2: Copywork

Copy and chunk the story. Look at the opposite page if you need help.

The tip of the feather is cut to

T

form a point. Then the shaft is

f

filled with ink. Learning to write

f

with a quill pen takes time and

w

practice. After every few words,

p

the pen runs out of ink. Then

t

you must refill it from an inkwell.

y

The ballpoint pens we have today

T

are much easier to use!

a

American Spirit Student 4B

4C
Section 1: Consonant Chunks

1. Read the story to your student.
2. Read it together slowly. Have the student look carefully at each word as you read.
3. Help your student look for and mark all the consonant chunks in blue.

In colonial times, people used quill pens to write. A quill is the hollow shaft inside a feather. The tip of the feather is cut to form a point. Then the shaft is filled with ink. Learning to write with a quill pen takes time and practice. After every few words, the pen runs out of ink. Then you must refill it from an inkwell. The ballpoint pens we have today are much easier to use!

Consonant Chunks

ch	gh	ph	sh	th	wh		
gn	kn	qu	wr	dg	ck	tch	
bb	cc	dd	ff	gg	hh	kk	ll	mm
nn	pp	rr	ss	tt	ww	vv	zz

Section 2: Copywork

Copy and chunk the story. Look at the opposite page if you need help.

In colonial times, people used

I

quill pens to write. A quill is the

q

hollow shaft inside a feather.

h

The tip of the feather is cut to

T

form a point. Then the shaft is

f

filled with ink. Learning to write

f

with a quill pen takes time and

w

practice. After every few words,

p

the pen runs out of ink.

t

American Spirit Student 4C

4D

Section 1: Consonant Chunks

1. Read the story to your student.
2. Read it together slowly. Have the student look carefully at each word as you read.
3. Together, find all the **consonant chunks** in the passage and mark them in blue.

In colonial times, people used quill pens to write. A quill is the hollow shaft inside a feather. The tip of the feather is cut to form a point. Then the shaft is filled with ink. Learning to write with a quill pen takes time and practice. After every few words, the pen runs out of ink. Then you must refill it from an inkwell. The ballpoint pens we have today are much easier to use!

Consonant Chunks

ch	gh	ph	sh	th	wh
gn	kn	qu	wr	dg	ck	tch
bb	cc	dd	ff	gg	hh	kk	ll	mm
nn	pp	rr	ss	tt	ww	vv	zz

Section 2: First Dictation

Write this week's story from dictation. Take your time and ask for help if you need it.

In

4E
Section 1: Consonant Chunks

1. Read the story to your student.
2. Read it together slowly. Have the student look carefully at each word as you read.
3. Together, find all the **consonant chunks** in the passage and mark them in blue.

In colonial times, people used quill pens to write. A quill is the hollow shaft inside a feather. The tip of the feather is cut to form a point. Then the shaft is filled with ink. Learning to write with a quill pen takes time and practice. After every few words, the pen runs out of ink. Then you must refill it from an inkwell. The ballpoint pens we have today are much easier to use!

Consonant Chunks

ch	gh	ph	sh	th	wh		
gn	kn	qu	wr	dg	ck	tch	
bb	cc	dd	ff	gg	hh	kk	ll	mm
nn	pp	rr	ss	tt	ww	vv	zz

American Spirit Student

Section 2: Second Dictation

See if you can write this week's story from dictation without asking for help.

5A
Section 1: Vowel and Consonant Chunks

1. Read the story to your student.
2. Read it together slowly. Have the student look carefully at each word as you read.
3. Together, find and mark all the **vowel chunks** and **consonant chunks**. Use yellow for <u>vowel chunks</u> and blue for <u>consonant chunks</u>.

As a young boy, Eli Whitney loved to tinker. He loved to see how things worked. When he was older, he invented a cotton gin. With the turn of a crank, steel teeth grabbed the fibers of cotton. The teeth pulled the fibers through holes and left the seeds behind. Before this, people had to separate the seeds by hand. With the gin, cotton could be produced faster. Soon cotton became the main crop of the South.

Vowel Chunks
aa ae ai ao au aw ay
ea ee ei eo ew ey eau
ia ie ii io iu
oa oe oi oo ou ow oy
ua ue ui uo uy

Consonant Chunks
ch gh ph sh th wh
gn kn qu wr dg ck tch
bb cc dd ff gg hh kk ll mm
nn pp rr ss tt ww vv zz

Section 2: Copywork
Copy and chunk the story.

As a young boy, Eli Whitney loved
to tinker. He loved to see how
things worked. When he was older,
he invented a cotton gin. With the
turn of a crank, steel teeth
grabbed the fibers of cotton. The
teeth pulled the fibers through
holes and left the seeds behind.

5B

Section 1: Vowel and Consonant Chunks

1. Read the story to your student.
2. Read it together slowly. Have the student look carefully at each word as you read.
3. Together, find and mark all the **vowel chunks** and **consonant chunks**. Use yellow for <u>vowel chunks</u> and blue for <u>**consonant chunks**</u>.

As a young boy, Eli Whitney loved to tinker. He loved to see how things worked. When he was older, he invented a cotton gin. With the turn of a crank, steel teeth grabbed the fibers of cotton. The teeth pulled the fibers through holes and left the seeds behind. Before this, people had to separate the seeds by hand. With the gin, cotton could be produced faster. Soon cotton became the main crop of the South.

Vowel Chunks

aa ae ai ao au aw ay
ea ee ei eo ew ey eau
ia ie ii io iu
oa oe oi oo ou ow oy
ua ue ui uo uy

Consonant Chunks

ch gh ph sh th wh
gn kn qu wr dg ck tch
bb cc dd ff gg hh kk ll mm
nn pp rr ss tt ww vv zz

Section 2: Copywork
Copy and chunk the story.

With the turn of a crank, steel
W
teeth grabbed the fibers of cotton.
t
The teeth pulled the fibers through
T
holes and left the seeds behind.
h
Before this, people had to separate
B
the seeds by hand. With the gin,
t
cotton could be produced faster.
c
Soon cotton became the main crop
S
of the South.
o

5C Section 1: Vowel and Consonant Chunks

1. Read the story to your student.
2. Read it together slowly. Have the student look carefully at each word as you read.
3. Together, find and mark all the **vowel chunks** and **consonant chunks**. Use yellow for <u>vowel chunks</u> and blue for <u>consonant chunks</u>.

As a young boy, Eli Whitney loved to tinker. He loved to see how things worked. When he was older, he invented a cotton gin. With the turn of a crank, steel teeth grabbed the fibers of cotton. The teeth pulled the fibers through holes and left the seeds behind. Before this, people had to separate the seeds by hand. With the gin, cotton could be produced faster. Soon cotton became the main crop of the South.

Vowel Chunks

aa	ae	ai	ao	au	aw	ay
ea	ee	ei	eo	ew	ey	eau
ia	ie	ii	io	iu		
oa	oe	oi	oo	ou	ow	oy
ua	ue	ui	uo	uy		

Consonant Chunks

ch	gh	ph	sh	th	wh	
gn	kn	qu	wr	dg	ck	tch
bb	cc	dd	ff	gg	hh	kk	ll	mm
nn	pp	rr	ss	tt	ww	vv	zz

Section 2: Copywork
Copy and chunk the story.

As a young boy, Eli Whitney loved
to tinker. He loved to see how
things worked. When he was older,
he invented a cotton gin. With the
turn of a crank, steel teeth
grabbed the fibers of cotton. The
teeth pulled the fibers through
holes and left the seeds behind.

5D

Section 1: Vowel and Consonant Chunks

1. Read the story to your student.
2. Read it together slowly. Have the student look carefully at each word as you read.
3. Together, find and mark all the **vowel chunks** and **consonant chunks**. Use yellow for <u>vowel chunks</u> and blue for <u>consonant chunks</u>.

As a young boy, Eli Whitney loved to tinker. He loved to see how things worked. When he was older, he invented a cotton gin. With the turn of a crank, steel teeth grabbed the fibers of cotton. The teeth pulled the fibers through holes and left the seeds behind. Before this, people had to separate the seeds by hand. With the gin, cotton could be produced faster. Soon cotton became the main crop of the South.

Vowel Chunks

aa ae ai ao au aw ay
ea ee ei eo ew ey eau
ia ie ii io iu
oa oe oi oo ou ow oy
ua ue ui uo uy

Consonant Chunks

ch gh ph sh th wh
gn kn qu wr dg ck tch
bb cc dd ff gg hh kk ll mm
nn pp rr ss tt ww vv zz

Section 2: First Dictation

Write this week's story from dictation. Take your time and ask for help if you need it.

As

5E

Section 1: Vowel and Consonant Chunks

1. Read the story to your student.
2. Read it together slowly. Have the student look carefully at each word as you read.
3. Together, find and mark all the **vowel chunks** and **consonant chunks**. Use yellow for <u>vowel chunks</u> and blue for <u>consonant chunks</u>.

As a young boy, Eli Whitney loved to tinker. He loved to see how things worked. When he was older, he invented a cotton gin. With the turn of a crank, steel teeth grabbed the fibers of cotton. The teeth pulled the fibers through holes and left the seeds behind. Before this, people had to separate the seeds by hand. With the gin, cotton could be produced faster. Soon cotton became the main crop of the South.

Vowel Chunks

aa ae ai ao au aw ay
ea ee ei eo ew ey eau
ia ie ii io iu
oa oe oi oo ou ow oy
ua ue ui uo uy

Consonant Chunks

ch gh ph sh th wh
gn kn qu wr dg ck tch
bb cc dd ff gg hh kk ll mm
nn pp rr ss tt ww vv zz

Section 2: Second Dictation

See if you can write this week's story from dictation without asking for help.

I spelled _____ words correctly.

6A

Section 1: Vowel and Consonant Chunks

1. Read the story to your student.
2. Read it together slowly. Have the student look carefully at each word as you read.
3. Together, find and mark all the **vowel chunks** and **consonant chunks**. Use yellow for <u>vowel chunks</u> and blue for <u>consonant chunks</u>.

In times past, building a barn by hand was too much work for one family. So they had a barn raising. People from all around would gather at a farm. There might be 100 men working together. Women cooked and served meals. Children helped in small ways. In just a day or two, they could build a large barn! It was hard work, but people had a chance to see and help each other.

Consonant Chunks

ch gh ph sh th wh
gn kn qu wr dg ck tch
bb cc dd ff gg hh kk ll mm
nn pp rr ss tt ww vv zz

Vowel Chunks

aa ae ai ao au aw ay
ea ee ei eo ew ey eau
ia ie ii io iu
oa oe oi oo ou ow oy
ua ue ui uo uy

Section 2: Copywork

Copy and chunk the story.

In times past, building a barn by
I

hand was too much work for one
h

family. So they had a barn raising.
f

People from all around would
P

gather at a farm. There might
g

be 100 men working together.
b

Women cooked and served meals.
W

Children helped in small ways.
C

6B

Section 1: Vowel and Consonant Chunks

1. Read the story to your student.
2. Read it together slowly. Have the student look carefully at each word as you read.
3. Together, find and mark all the **vowel chunks** and **consonant chunks**. Use yellow for <u>vowel chunks</u> and blue for <u>consonant chunks</u>.

In times past, building a barn by hand was too much work for one family. So they had a barn raising. People from all around would gather at a farm. There might be 100 men working together. Women cooked and served meals. Children helped in small ways. In just a day or two, they could build a large barn! It was hard work, but people had a chance to see and help each other.

Consonant Chunks

ch	gh	ph	sh	th	wh
gn	kn	qu	wr	dg	ck	tch
bb	cc	dd	ff	gg	hh	kk	ll	mm
nn	pp	rr	ss	tt	ww	vv	zz

Vowel Chunks

aa	ae	ai	ao	au	aw	ay
ea	ee	ei	eo	ew	ey	eau
ia	ie	ii	io	iu
oa	oe	oi	oo	ou	ow	oy
ua	ue	ui	uo	uy

56   American Spirit Student

Section 2: Copywork
Copy and chunk the story.

People from all around would
P

gather at a farm. There might be
g

100 men working together. Women
100

cooked and served meals.
c

Children helped in small ways.
C

In just a day or two, they could
I

build a large barn! It was hard
b

work, but people had a chance
w

to see and help each other.
t

6C Section 1: Vowel and Consonant Chunks

1. Read the story to your student.
2. Read it together slowly. Have the student look carefully at each word as you read.
3. Together, find and mark all the **vowel chunks** and **consonant chunks**. Use yellow for <u>vowel chunks</u> and blue for <u>consonant chunks</u>.

In times past, building a barn by hand was too much work for one family. So they had a barn raising. People from all around would gather at a farm. There might be 100 men working together. Women cooked and served meals. Children helped in small ways. In just a day or two, they could build a large barn! It was hard work, but people had a chance to see and help each other.

Consonant Chunks

ch	gh	ph	sh	th	wh
gn	kn	qu	wr	dg	ck	tch
bb	cc	dd	ff	gg	hh	kk	ll	mm
nn	pp	rr	ss	tt	ww	vv	zz

Vowel Chunks

aa	ae	ai	ao	au	aw	ay
ea	ee	ei	eo	ew	ey	eau
ia	ie	ii	io	iu
oa	oe	oi	oo	ou	ow	oy
ua	ue	ui	uo	uy

Section 2: Copywork

Copy and chunk the story.

In times past, building a barn by

I

hand was too much work for one

h

family. So they had a barn raising.

f

People from all around would

P

gather at a farm. There might

g

be 100 men working together.

b

Women cooked and served meals.

W

Children helped in small ways.

C

6D

Section 1: Vowel and Consonant Chunks

1. Read the story to your student.
2. Read it together slowly. Have the student look carefully at each word as you read.
3. Together, find and mark all the **vowel chunks** and **consonant chunks**. Use yellow for <u>vowel chunks</u> and blue for <u>consonant chunks</u>.

In times past, building a barn by hand was too much work for one family. So they had a barn raising. People from all around would gather at a farm. There might be 100 men working together. Women cooked and served meals. Children helped in small ways. In just a day or two, they could build a large barn! It was hard work, but people had a chance to see and help each other.

Consonant Chunks

ch	gh	ph	sh	th	wh		
gn	kn	qu	wr	dg	ck	tch	
bb	cc	dd	ff	gg	hh	kk	ll	mm
nn	pp	rr	ss	tt	ww	vv	zz

Vowel Chunks

aa	ae	ai	ao	au	aw	ay
ea	ee	ei	eo	ew	ey	eau
ia	ie	ii	io	iu		
oa	oe	oi	oo	ou	ow	oy
ua	ue	ui	uo	uy		

Section 2: First Dictation

Write this week's story from dictation. Take your time and ask for help if you need it.

In

American Spirit Student 6D   **I spelled _____ words correctly.**

6E
Section 1: Vowel and Consonant Chunks

1. Read the story to your student.
2. Read it together slowly. Have the student look carefully at each word as you read.
3. Together, find and mark all the **vowel chunks** and **consonant chunks**. Use yellow for <u>vowel chunks</u> and blue for <u>consonant chunks</u>.

In times past, building a barn by hand was too much work for one family. So they had a barn raising. People from all around would gather at a farm. There might be 100 men working together. Women cooked and served meals. Children helped in small ways. In just a day or two, they could build a large barn! It was hard work, but people had a chance to see and help each other.

Consonant Chunks
ch gh ph sh th wh
gn kn qu wr dg ck tch
bb cc dd ff gg hh kk ll mm
nn pp rr ss tt ww vv zz

Vowel Chunks
aa ae ai ao au aw ay
ea ee ei eo ew ey eau
ia ie ii io iu
oa oe oi oo ou ow oy
ua ue ui uo uy

Section 2: Second Dictation

See if you can write this week's story from dictation without asking for help.

I spelled _____ words correctly.

Section 1: Bossy r Chunks

1. Read the story to your student.

2. Read it together slowly. Have the student look carefully at each word as you read.

3. Go to the instructions for Lesson 7 in the *Handbook* for examples of how Bossy *r* changes the sound of a vowel. Together, look for **Bossy *r* chunks** and mark them in purple.

It took Patrick a while to figure out what kind of work to do. He tried farming, but his farm had poor soil. He started a store, but that did not go well. Finally he became a lawyer. In time, he became a great speaker. He gave stirring speeches about wanting freedom from England. Patrick Henry is remembered for ending one speech with the line, "Give me liberty, or give me death!"

Bossy r Chunks
ar   er   ir   or   ur

Section 2: Copywork

Copy the story. Mark all the Bossy *r* chunks on your copy.

It took Patrick a while to figure
out what kind of work to do.
He tried farming, but his farm
had poor soil. He started a store,
but that did not go well. Finally
he became a lawyer. In time, he
became a great speaker. He gave
stirring speeches about wanting
freedom from England.

American Spirit Student 7A

7B

Section 1: Bossy r Chunks

1. Read the story to your student.
2. Read it together slowly. Have the student look carefully at each word as you read.
3. Help your student find and mark the **Bossy r chunks** in purple.

It took Patrick a while to figure out what kind of work to do. He tried farming, but his farm had poor soil. He started a store, but that did not go well. Finally he became a lawyer. In time, he became a great speaker. He gave stirring speeches about wanting freedom from England. Patrick Henry is remembered for ending one speech with the line, "Give me liberty, or give me death!"

Bossy r Chunks
ar   er   ir   or   ur

Section 2: Copywork

Copy the story. Mark all the Bossy *r* chunks on your copy.

He started a store, but that did
not go well. Finally he became
a lawyer. In time, he became a
great speaker. He gave stirring
speeches about wanting freedom
from England. Patrick Henry is
remembered for ending one
speech with the line, "Give me
liberty, or give me death!"

7C

Section 1: Bossy r Chunks

1. Read the story to your student.
2. Read it together slowly. Have the student look carefully at each word as you read.
3. Help your student find and mark the **Bossy r chunks** in purple.

It took Patrick a while to figure out what kind of work to do. He tried farming, but his farm had poor soil. He started a store, but that did not go well. Finally he became a lawyer. In time, he became a great speaker. He gave stirring speeches about wanting freedom from England. Patrick Henry is remembered for ending one speech with the line, "Give me liberty, or give me death!"

Bossy r Chunks
ar   er   ir   or   ur

Section 2: Copywork

Copy the story. Mark all the Bossy *r* chunks on your copy.

It took Patrick a while to figure

out what kind of work to do.

He tried farming, but his farm

had poor soil. He started a store,

but that did not go well. Finally

he became a lawyer. In time, he

became a great speaker. He gave

stirring speeches about wanting

freedom from England.

7D

Section 1: Bossy r Chunks

1. Read the story to your student.
2. Read it together slowly. Have the student look carefully at each word as you read.
3. Help your student find and mark the **Bossy r chunks** in purple.

It took Patrick a while to figure out what kind of work to do. He tried farming, but his farm had poor soil. He started a store, but that did not go well. Finally he became a lawyer. In time, he became a great speaker. He gave stirring speeches about wanting freedom from England. Patrick Henry is remembered for ending one speech with the line, "Give me liberty, or give me death!"

Bossy r Chunks
ar   er   ir   or   ur

Section 2: First Dictation

Write this week's story from dictation. Take your time and ask for help if you need it.

It

7E

Section 1: Bossy r Chunks

1. Read the story to your student.
2. Read it together slowly. Have the student look carefully at each word as you read.
3. Help your student find and mark the **Bossy r chunks** in purple.

It took Patrick a while to figure out what kind of work to do. He tried farming, but his farm had poor soil. He started a store, but that did not go well. Finally he became a lawyer. In time, he became a great speaker. He gave stirring speeches about wanting freedom from England. Patrick Henry is remembered for ending one speech with the line, "Give me liberty, or give me death!"

Bossy r Chunks
ar   er   ir   or   ur

Section 2: Second Dictation

See if you can write this week's story from dictation without asking for help.

I spelled _____ words correctly.

8A

Section 1: Bossy r Chunks

1. Read the story to your student.
2. Read it together slowly. Have the student look carefully at each word as you read.
3. Together, look for **Bossy *r* chunks** and mark them in purple.

In 1775 David Bushnell built a one-man submarine. He called it the *Turtle* because of the way it looked. He used it to target enemy ships. His plan was to put a bomb on the hull of a large ship. Then he would escape through the murky water before the bomb blew up. His idea did not work very well. The *Turtle* is remembered as the first submarine used in a war.

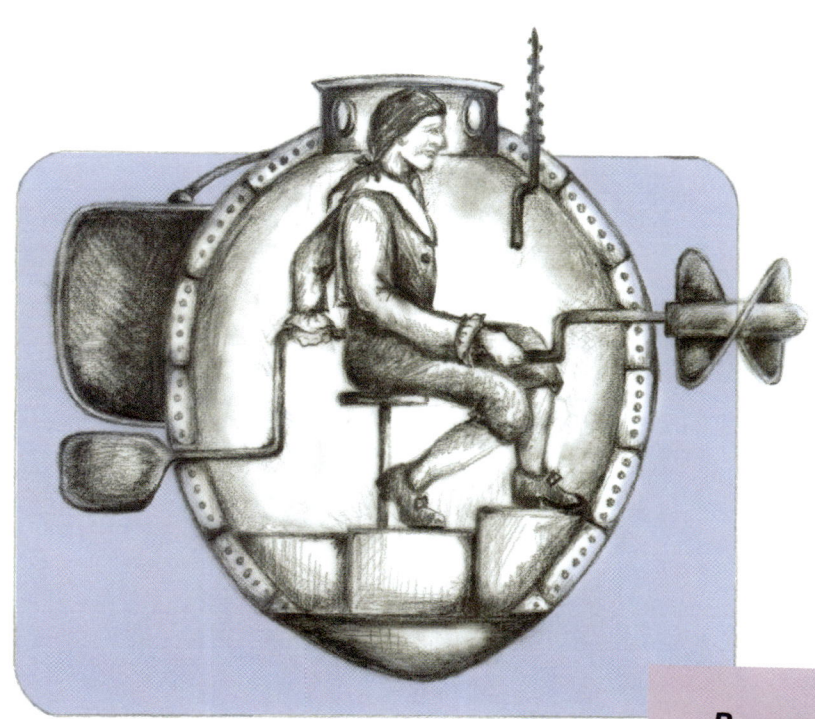

Bossy r Chunks
ar   er   ir   or   ur

Section 2: Copywork

Copy the story. Mark all the Bossy *r* chunks on your copy.

In 1775 David Bushnell built a
one-man submarine. He called it
the Turtle because of the way it
looked. He used it to target
enemy ships. His plan was to
put a bomb on the hull of a
large ship. Then he would escape
through the murky water
before the bomb blew up.

8B
Section 1: Bossy r Chunks

1. Read the story to your student.
2. Read it together slowly. Have the student look carefully at each word as you read.
3. Together, look for **Bossy *r* chunks** and mark them in purple.

In 1775 David Bushnell built a one-man submarine. He called it the *Turtle* because of the way it looked. He used it to target enemy ships. His plan was to put a bomb on the hull of a large ship. Then he would escape through the murky water before the bomb blew up. His idea did not work very well. The *Turtle* is remembered as the first submarine used in a war.

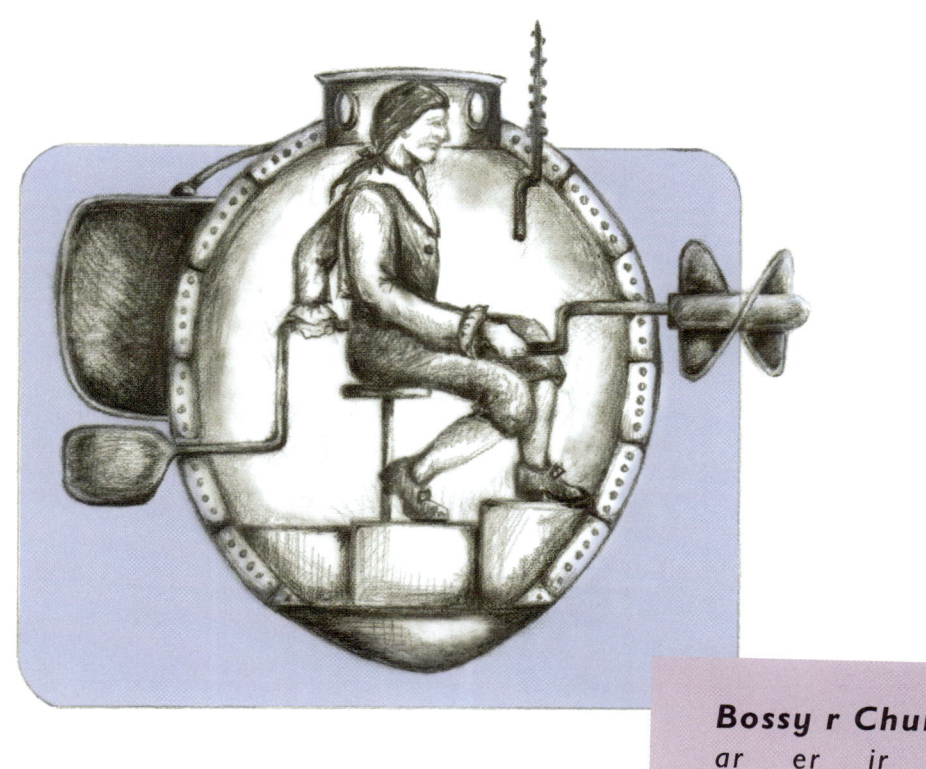

Bossy r Chunks
ar er ir or ur

Section 2: Copywork

Copy the story. Mark all the Bossy *r* chunks on your copy.

He used it to target enemy ships.

His plan was to put a bomb on

the hull of a large ship. Then he

would escape through the murky

water before the bomb blew up.

His idea did not work very well.

The Turtle is remembered as the

first submarine used in a war.

8C

Section 1: Bossy *r* Chunks

1. Read the story to your student.
2. Read it together slowly. Have the student look carefully at each word as you read.
3. Together, look for **Bossy *r* chunks** and mark them in purple.

In 1775 David Bushnell built a one-man submarine. He called it the *Turtle* because of the way it looked. He used it to target enemy ships. His plan was to put a bomb on the hull of a large ship. Then he would escape through the murky water before the bomb blew up. His idea did not work very well. The *Turtle* is remembered as the first submarine used in a war.

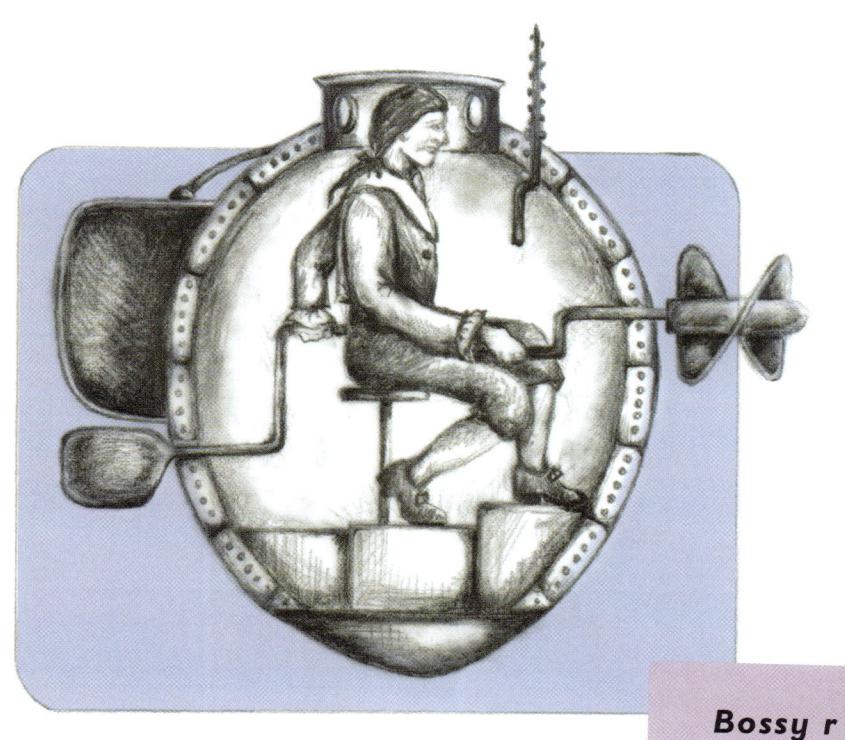

Bossy r Chunks
ar   er   ir   or   ur

Section 2: Copywork

Copy the story. Mark all the Bossy *r* chunks on your copy.

In 1775 David Bushnell built a
one-man submarine. He called it
the Turtle because of the way it
looked. He used it to target
enemy ships. His plan was to
put a bomb on the hull of a
large ship. Then he would escape
through the murky water
before the bomb blew up.

8D

Section 1: Bossy r Chunks

1. Read the story to your student.
2. Read it together slowly. Have the student look carefully at each word as you read.
3. Together, look for **Bossy *r* chunks** and mark them in purple.

In 1775 David Bushnell built a one-man submarine. He called it the *Turtle* because of the way it looked. He used it to target enemy ships. His plan was to put a bomb on the hull of a large ship. Then he would escape through the murky water before the bomb blew up. His idea did not work very well. The *Turtle* is remembered as the first submarine used in a war.

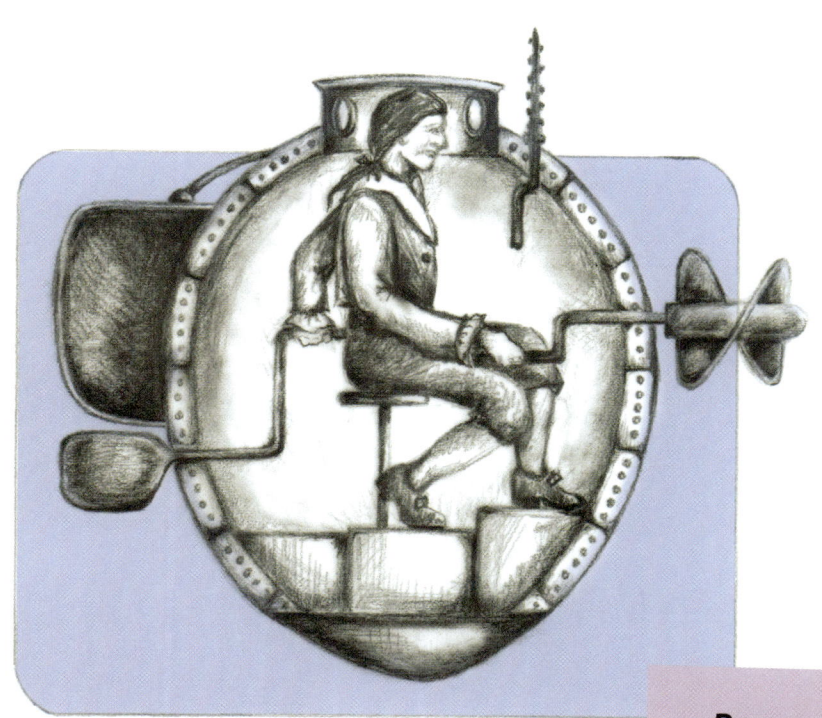

Bossy r Chunks
ar   er   ir   or   ur

Section 2: First Dictation

Write this week's story from dictation. Take your time and ask for help if you need it.

In

I spelled _____ words correctly.

8E
Section 1: Bossy r Chunks

1. Read the story to your student.
2. Read it together slowly. Have the student look carefully at each word as you read.
3. Together, look for **Bossy *r* chunks** and mark them in purple.

In 1775 David Bushnell built a one-man submarine. He called it the *Turtle* because of the way it looked. He used it to target enemy ships. His plan was to put a bomb on the hull of a large ship. Then he would escape through the murky water before the bomb blew up. His idea did not work very well. The *Turtle* is remembered as the first submarine used in a war.

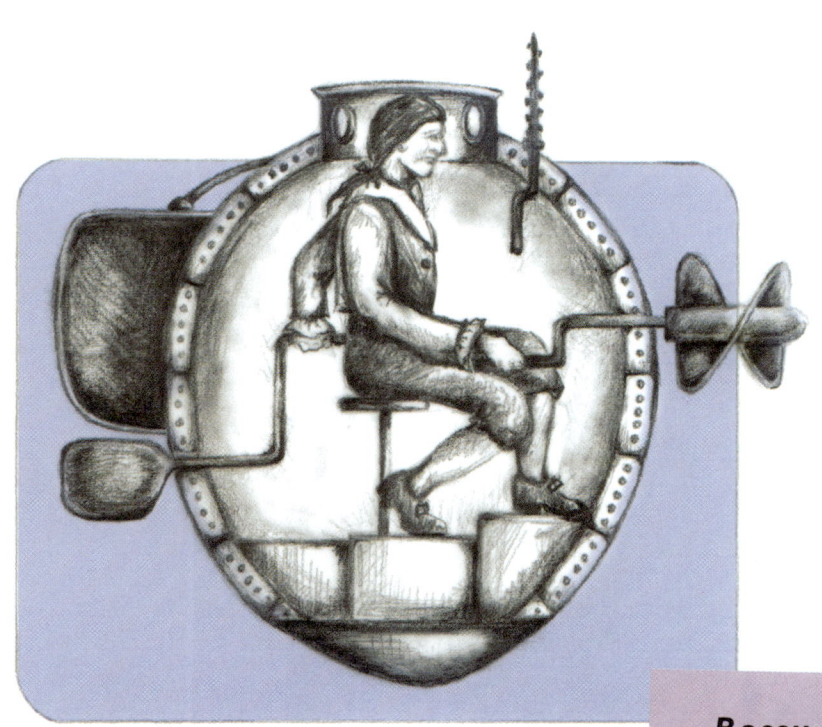

Bossy r Chunks
ar   er   ir   or   ur

82 American Spirit Student

Section 2: Second Dictation

See if you can write this week's story from dictation without asking for help.

Section 1: Vowel, Consonant, and Bossy r Chunks

1. Read the story to your student.
2. Read it together slowly. Have the student look carefully at each word as you read.
3. This week, look for all the letter patterns studied so far. Mark **vowel chunks** in yellow, **consonant chunks** in blue, and **Bossy r chunks** in purple. The word *soldier* has overlapping chunks. We suggest that you have your student mark the **vowel chunk** rather than the **Bossy r chunk**.

A few women helped fight in the Revolutionary War. Soldiers fighting battles need water. Often a woman would run back and forth from a spring. In one battle, a soldier fell to the ground. His wife, Mary Hays, dropped her pitcher. She took over firing the cannon. Over and over she loaded and fired. Suddenly a cannon ball whizzed right between her legs! It tore the bottom of her skirt, but she was not hurt. She kept on fighting.

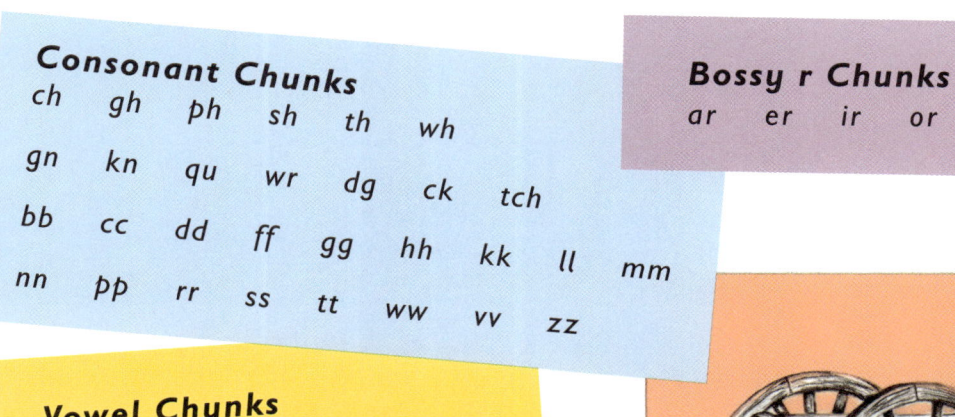

Section 2: Copywork
Copy and chunk the story.

A few women helped fight in
the Revolutionary War. Soldiers
fighting battles need water. Often
a woman would run back and
forth from a spring. In one battle,
a soldier fell to the ground. His
wife, Mary Hays, dropped her
pitcher. She took over firing the
cannon.

9B

Section 1: Vowel, Consonant, and Bossy *r* Chunks

1. Read the story to your student.
2. Read it together slowly. Have the student look carefully at each word as you read.
3. Together, mark **vowel chunks** in yellow, **consonant chunks** in blue, and **Bossy *r* chunks** in purple.

A few women helped fight in the Revolutionary War. Soldiers fighting battles need water. Often a woman would run back and forth from a spring. In one battle, a soldier fell to the ground. His wife, Mary Hays, dropped her pitcher. She took over firing the cannon. Over and over she loaded and fired. Suddenly a cannon ball whizzed right between her legs! It tore the bottom of her skirt, but she was not hurt. She kept on fighting.

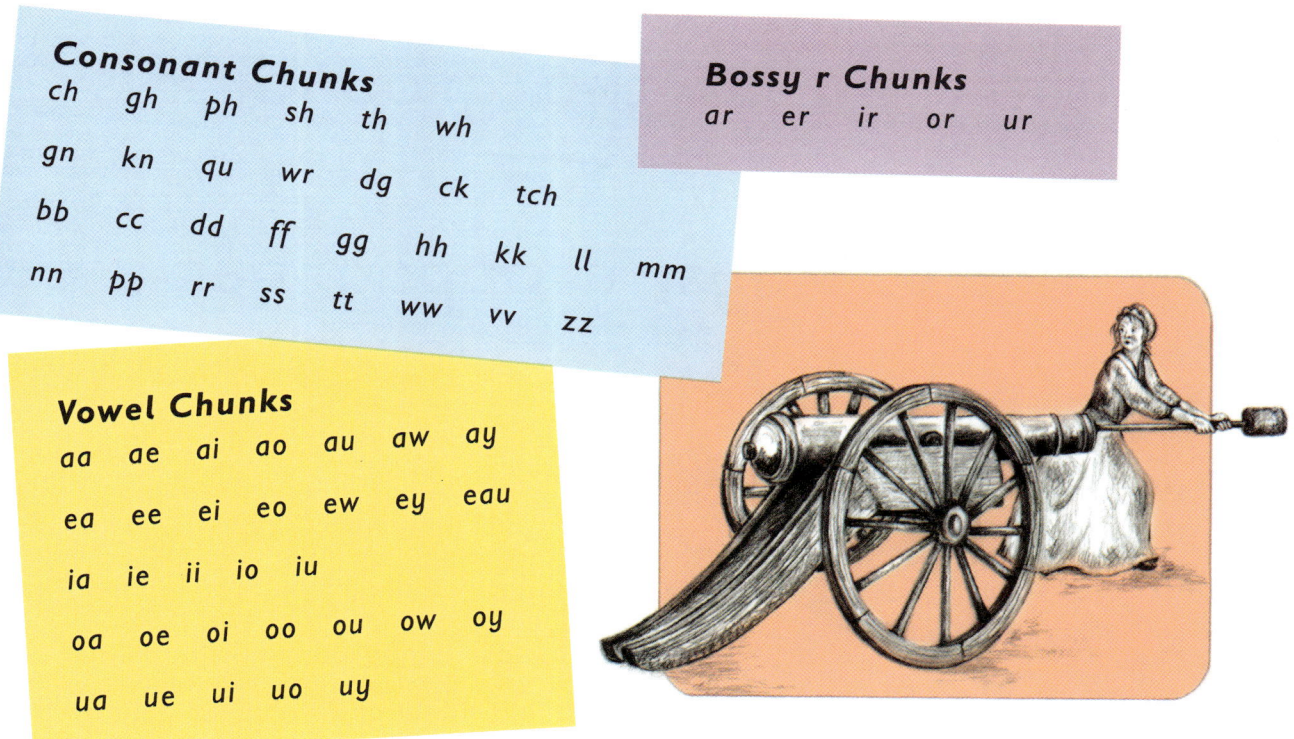

Consonant Chunks

ch gh ph sh th wh
gn kn qu wr dg ck tch
bb cc dd ff gg hh kk ll mm
nn pp rr ss tt ww vv zz

Bossy r Chunks

ar er ir or ur

Vowel Chunks

aa ae ai ao au aw ay
ea ee ei eo ew ey eau
ia ie ii io iu
oa oe oi oo ou ow oy
ua ue ui uo uy

American Spirit Student

Section 2: Copywork

Copy and chunk the story.

In one battle, a soldier fell to
I
the ground. His wife, Mary Hays,
t
dropped her pitcher. She took over
d
firing the cannon. Over and over
f
she loaded and fired. Suddenly a
s
cannon ball whizzed right between
c
her legs! It tore the bottom of
h
her skirt, but she was not hurt.
h
She kept on fighting.
S

9C

Section 1: **Vowel, Consonant, and Bossy r Chunks**

1. Read the story to your student.
2. Read it together slowly. Have the student look carefully at each word as you read.
3. Together, mark **vowel chunks** in yellow, **consonant chunks** in blue, and **Bossy r chunks** in purple.

A few women helped fight in the Revolutionary War. Soldiers fighting battles need water. Often a woman would run back and forth from a spring. In one battle, a soldier fell to the ground. His wife, Mary Hays, dropped her pitcher. She took over firing the cannon. Over and over she loaded and fired. Suddenly a cannon ball whizzed right between her legs! It tore the bottom of her skirt, but she was not hurt. She kept on fighting.

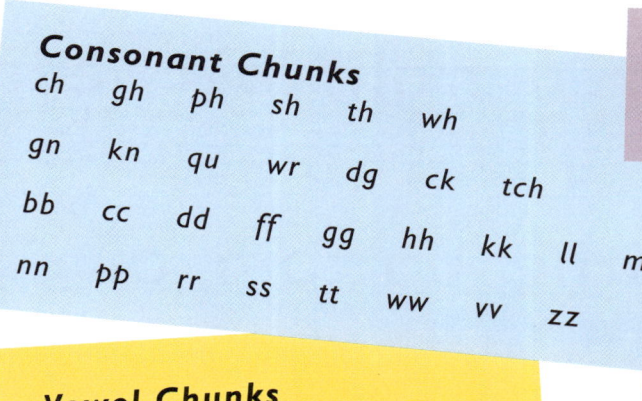

Consonant Chunks
ch gh ph sh th wh
gn kn qu wr dg ck tch
bb cc dd ff gg hh kk ll mm
nn pp rr ss tt ww vv zz

Bossy r Chunks
ar er ir or ur

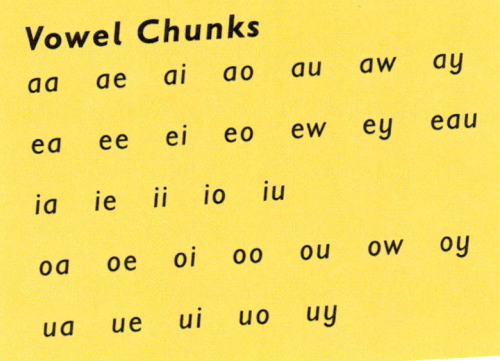

Vowel Chunks
aa ae ai ao au aw ay
ea ee ei eo ew ey eau
ia ie ii io iu
oa oe oi oo ou ow oy
ua ue ui uo uy

Section 2: Copywork

Copy and chunk the story.

A few women helped fight in

A

the Revolutionary War. Soldiers

t

fighting battles need water. Often

f

a woman would run back and

a

forth from a spring. In one battle,

f

a soldier fell to the ground. His

a

wife, Mary Hays, dropped her

w

pitcher. She took over firing the

p

cannon.

c

9D

Section 1: Vowel, Consonant, and Bossy r Chunks

1. Read the story to your student.
2. Read it together slowly. Have the student look carefully at each word as you read.
3. Together, mark **vowel chunks** in yellow, **consonant chunks** in blue, and **Bossy r chunks** in purple.

A few women helped fight in the Revolutionary War. Soldiers fighting battles need water. Often a woman would run back and forth from a spring. In one battle, a soldier fell to the ground. His wife, Mary Hays, dropped her pitcher. She took over firing the cannon. Over and over she loaded and fired. Suddenly a cannon ball whizzed right between her legs! It tore the bottom of her skirt, but she was not hurt. She kept on fighting.

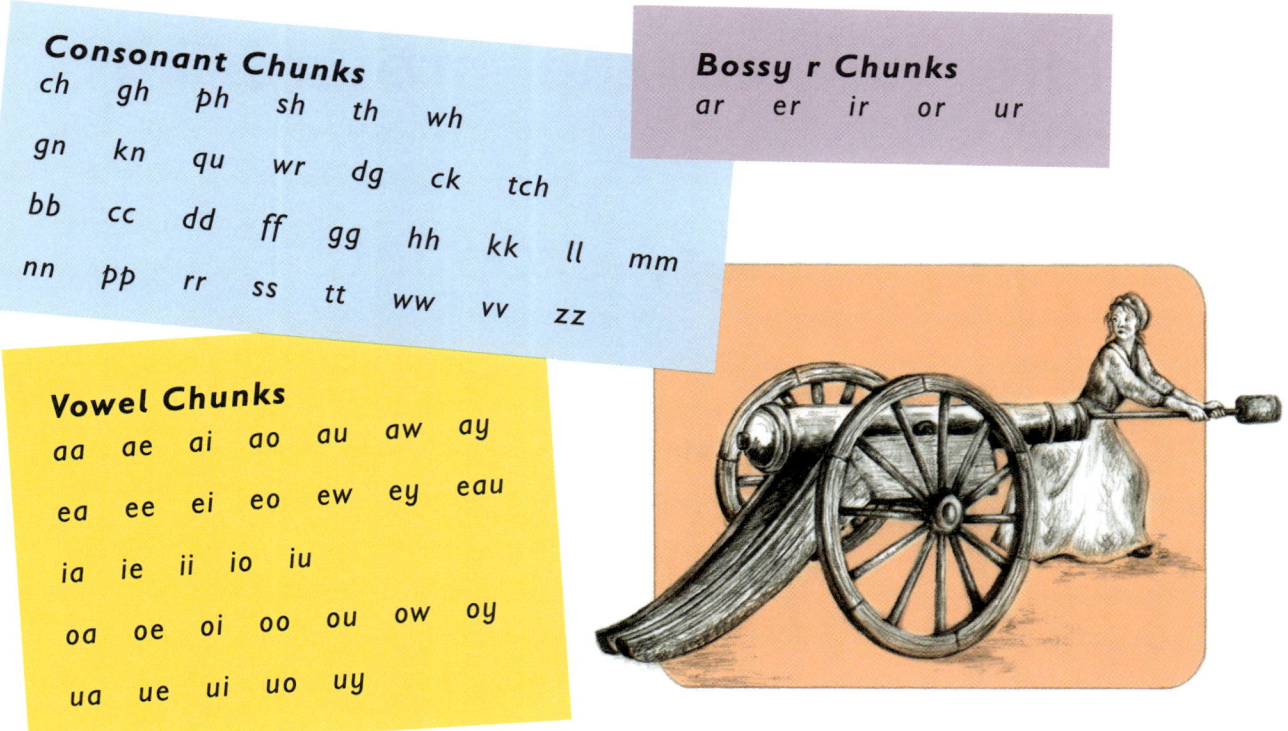

Consonant Chunks
ch gh ph sh th wh
gn kn qu wr dg ck tch
bb cc dd ff gg hh kk ll mm
nn pp rr ss tt ww vv zz

Bossy r Chunks
ar er ir or ur

Vowel Chunks
aa ae ai ao au aw ay
ea ee ei eo ew ey eau
ia ie ii io iu
oa oe oi oo ou ow oy
ua ue ui uo uy

American Spirit Student

Section 2: First Dictation

Write this week's story from dictation. Take your time and ask for help if you need it.

A

9E

Section 1: Vowel, Consonant, and Bossy r Chunks

1. Read the story to your student.
2. Read it together slowly. Have the student look carefully at each word as you read.
3. Together, mark **vowel chunks** in yellow, **consonant chunks** in blue, and **Bossy r chunks** in purple.

A few women helped fight in the Revolutionary War. Soldiers fighting battles need water. Often a woman would run back and forth from a spring. In one battle, a soldier fell to the ground. His wife, Mary Hays, dropped her pitcher. She took over firing the cannon. Over and over she loaded and fired. Suddenly a cannon ball whizzed right between her legs! It tore the bottom of her skirt, but she was not hurt. She kept on fighting.

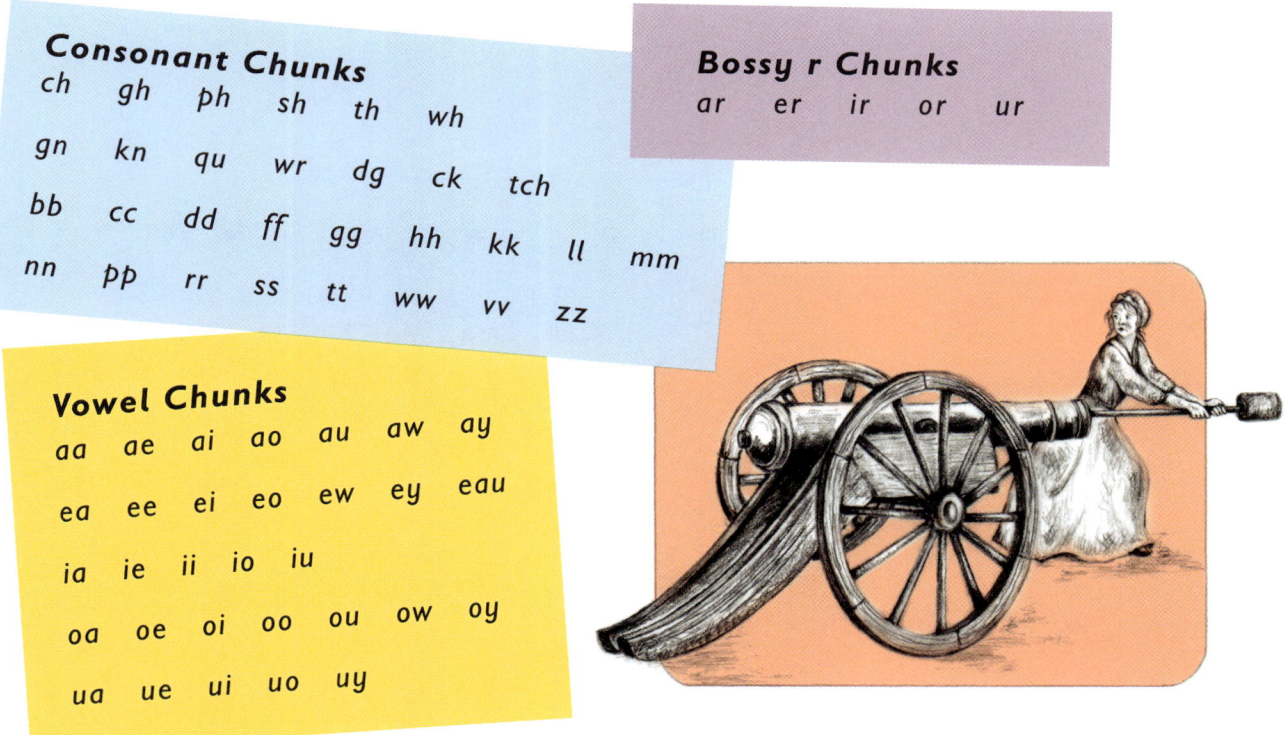

Consonant Chunks
ch gh ph sh th wh
gn kn qu wr dg ck tch
bb cc dd ff gg hh kk ll mm
nn pp rr ss tt ww vv zz

Bossy r Chunks
ar er ir or ur

Vowel Chunks
aa ae ai ao au aw ay
ea ee ei eo ew ey eau
ia ie ii io iu
oa oe oi oo ou ow oy
ua ue ui uo uy

American Spirit Student

Section 2: Second Dictation

See if you can write this week's story from dictation without asking for help.

10A

Section 1: Vowel, Consonant, and Bossy *r* Chunks

1. Read the story to your student.
2. Read it together slowly. Have the student look carefully at each word as you read.
3. Together, mark the **vowel chunks**, **consonant chunks**, and **Bossy *r* chunks**. Be sure to use the correct color for each letter pattern.

Annie Oakley was skilled with a rifle. As a teenager, she shot game to feed her family. She sold the extra. Soon she paid off her family's debt. People noticed her shooting skill. She became a sharpshooter in Buffalo Bill's Wild West Show. She was only five feet tall, so she was called Little Sure Shot. She performed with her husband and set many records for shooting.

Bossy *r* Chunks
ar er ir or ur

Vowel Chunks
aa ae ai ao au aw ay
ea ee ei eo ew ey eau
ia ie ii io iu
oa oe oi oo ou ow oy
ua ue ui uo uy

Consonant Chunks
ch gh ph sh th wh
gn kn qu wr dg ck tch
bb cc dd ff gg hh kk ll mm
nn pp rr ss tt ww vv zz

Section 2: Copywork

Copy and chunk the story.

Annie Oakley was skilled with
A
a rifle. As a teenager, she shot
a
game to feed her family. She sold
g
the extra. Soon she paid off her
t
family's debt. People noticed her
f
shooting skill. She became a
s
sharpshooter in Buffalo Bill's Wild
s
West Show.
W

10B Section 1: Vowel, Consonant, and Bossy r Chunks

1. Read the story to your student.
2. Read it together slowly. Have the student look carefully at each word as you read.
3. Together, mark the **vowel chunks**, **consonant chunks**, and **Bossy r chunks**. Be sure to use the correct color for each letter pattern.

Annie Oakley was skilled with a rifle. As a teenager, she shot game to feed her family. She sold the extra. Soon she paid off her family's debt. People noticed her shooting skill. She became a sharpshooter in Buffalo Bill's Wild West Show. She was only five feet tall, so she was called Little Sure Shot. She performed with her husband and set many records for shooting.

Bossy r Chunks
ar er ir or ur

Vowel Chunks
aa ae ai ao au aw ay
ea ee ei eo ew ey eau
ia ie ii io iu
oa oe oi oo ou ow oy
ua ue ui uo uy

Consonant Chunks
ch gh ph sh th wh
gn kn qu wr dg ck tch
bb cc dd ff gg hh kk ll mm
nn pp rr ss tt ww vv zz

Section 2: Copywork

Copy and chunk the story.

She sold the extra. Soon she paid
off her family's debt. People
noticed her shooting skill. She
became a sharpshooter in Buffalo
Bill's Wild West Show. She was
only five feet tall, so she was
called Little Sure Shot. She
performed with her husband and
set many records for shooting.

10C

Section 1: Vowel, Consonant, and Bossy r Chunks

1. Read the story to your student.
2. Read it together slowly. Have the student look carefully at each word as you read.
3. Together, mark the <u>**vowel chunks**</u>, <u>**consonant chunks**</u>, and <u>**Bossy *r* chunks**</u>. Be sure to use the correct color for each letter pattern.

Annie Oakley was skilled with a rifle. As a teenager, she shot game to feed her family. She sold the extra. Soon she paid off her family's debt. People noticed her shooting skill. She became a sharpshooter in Buffalo Bill's Wild West Show. She was only five feet tall, so she was called Little Sure Shot. She performed with her husband and set many records for shooting.

Bossy r Chunks
ar   er   ir   or   ur

Vowel Chunks
aa ae ai ao au aw ay
ea ee ei eo ew ey eau
ia ie ii io iu
oa oe oi oo ou ow oy
ua ue ui uo uy

Consonant Chunks
ch gh ph sh th wh
gn kn qu wr dg ck tch
bb cc dd ff gg hh kk ll mm
nn pp rr ss tt ww vv zz

98   *American Spirit Student*

Section 2: Copywork

Copy and chunk the story.

Annie Oakley was skilled with
A

a rifle. As a teenager, she shot
a

game to feed her family. She sold
g

the extra. Soon she paid off her
t

family's debt. People noticed her
f

shooting skill. She became a
s

sharpshooter in Buffalo Bill's Wild
s

West Show.
W

10D

Section 1: Vowel, Consonant, and Bossy r Chunks

1. Read the story to your student.
2. Read it together slowly. Have the student look carefully at each word as you read.
3. Together, mark the <u>vowel chunks</u>, <u>consonant chunks</u>, and <u>**Bossy *r* chunks**</u>. Be sure to use the correct color for each letter pattern.

Annie Oakley was skilled with a rifle. As a teenager, she shot game to feed her family. She sold the extra. Soon she paid off her family's debt. People noticed her shooting skill. She became a sharpshooter in Buffalo Bill's Wild West Show. She was only five feet tall, so she was called Little Sure Shot. She performed with her husband and set many records for shooting.

Bossy r Chunks
ar   er   ir   or   ur

Vowel Chunks
aa   ae   ai   ao   au   aw   ay
ea   ee   ei   eo   ew   ey   eau
ia   ie   ii   io   iu
oa   oe   oi   oo   ou   ow   oy
ua   ue   ui   uo   uy

Consonant Chunks
ch   gh   ph   sh   th   wh
gn   kn   qu   wr   dg   ck   tch
bb   cc   dd   ff   gg   hh   kk   ll   mm
nn   pp   rr   ss   tt   ww   vv   zz

American Spirit Student

Section 2: First Dictation

Write this week's story from dictation. Take your time and ask for help if you need it.

Annie

10E

Section 1: Vowel, Consonant, and Bossy *r* Chunks

1. Read the story to your student.
2. Read it together slowly. Have the student look carefully at each word as you read.
3. Together, mark the <u>vowel chunks</u>, <u>consonant chunks</u>, and <u>Bossy *r* chunks</u>. Be sure to use the correct color for each letter pattern.

Annie Oakley was skilled with a rifle. As a teenager, she shot game to feed her family. She sold the extra. Soon she paid off her family's debt. People noticed her shooting skill. She became a sharpshooter in Buffalo Bill's Wild West Show. She was only five feet tall, so she was called Little Sure Shot. She performed with her husband and set many records for shooting.

Bossy r Chunks
ar   er   ir   or   ur

Vowel Chunks
aa ae ai ao au aw ay
ea ee ei eo ew ey eau
ia ie ii io iu
oa oe oi oo ou ow oy
ua ue ui uo uy

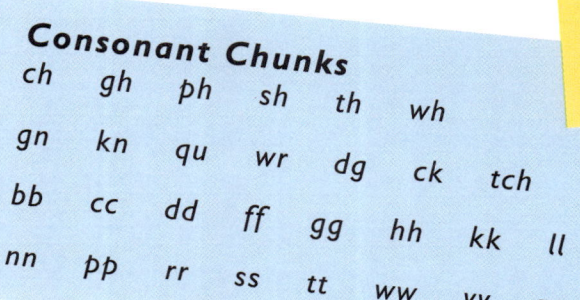

Section 2: Second Dictation

See if you can write this week's story from dictation without asking for help.

11A Section 1: Tricky *y* Guy, Endings, Silent Letters

1. Read the story to your student.

2. Read it together slowly. Have the student look carefully at each word as you read.

3. In this lesson, you will be finding three new letter patterns. They are **Tricky *y* Guy**, **endings**, and **silent letters**. We recommend that you mark **endings** before **silent letters**. Look for **silent letters** that are not part of **endings** or other chunks.

4. Mark **Tricky y Guy** in green, **endings** in pink or red, and **silent letters** in orange.

5. Refer to the *Handbook* for more information about these letter patterns.

Samuel Morse loved painting. He painted pictures of famous people. Later in life he tried to find a faster way to send messages. He invented a telegraph. It used Morse code, a system of dots and dashes. Each letter and number had its own code. Messages that would have taken weeks to send by mail could now be sent quickly over wires.

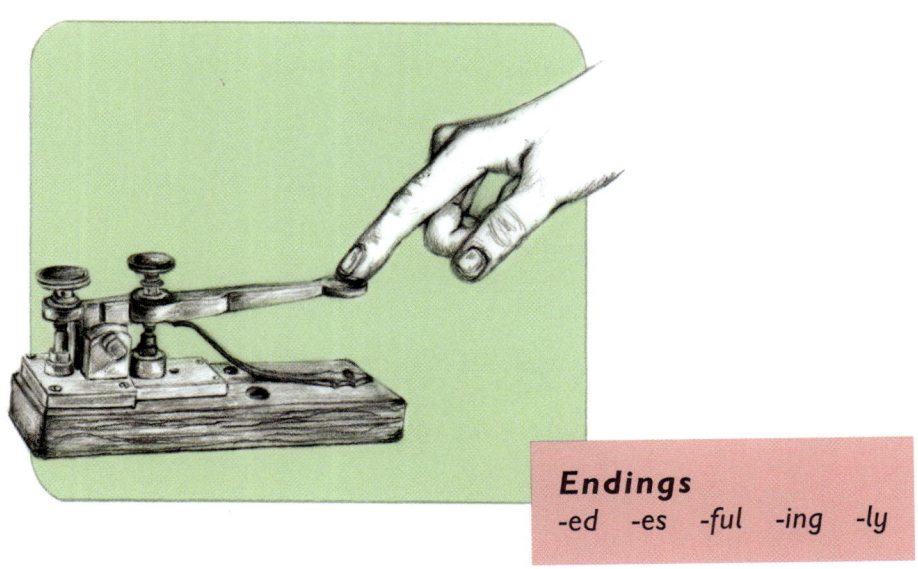

Endings
-ed -es -ful -ing -ly

American Spirit Student

Section 2: Copywork
Copy and chunk the story.

Samuel Morse loved painting.
S
He painted pictures of famous
H
people. Later in life he tried to
P
find a faster way to send
f
messages. He invented a telegraph.
m
It used Morse code, a system
I
of dots and dashes. Each letter
o
and number had its own code.
a

American Spirit Student 11A

11B
Section 1: Tricky y Guy, Endings, Silent Letters

1. Read the story to your student.
2. Read it together slowly. Have the student look carefully at each word as you read.
3. Mark **Tricky *y* Guy** in green, **endings** in pink or red, and **silent letters** in orange.

Samuel Morse loved painting. He painted pictures of famous people. Later in life he tried to find a faster way to send messages. He invented a telegraph. It used Morse code, a system of dots and dashes. Each letter and number had its own code. Messages that would have taken weeks to send by mail could now be sent quickly over wires.

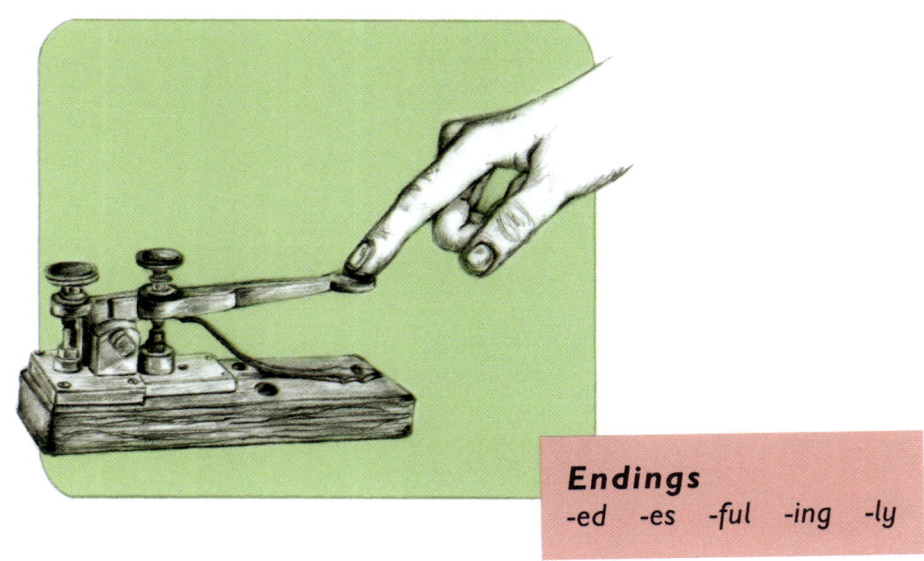

Endings
-ed -es -ful -ing -ly

Section 2: Copywork
Copy and chunk the story.

Later in life he tried to find a
L

faster way to send messages.
f

He invented a telegraph. It used
H

Morse code, a system of dots and
M

dashes. Each letter and number
d

had its own code. Messages that
h

would have taken weeks to send
w

by mail could now be sent quickly
b

over wires.
o

11C

Section 1: Tricky y Guy, Endings, Silent Letters

1. Read the story to your student.
2. Read it together slowly. Have the student look carefully at each word as you read.
3. Mark **Tricky *y* Guy** in green, **endings** in pink or red, and **silent letters** in orange.

Samuel Morse loved painting. He painted pictures of famous people. Later in life he tried to find a faster way to send messages. He invented a telegraph. It used Morse code, a system of dots and dashes. Each letter and number had its own code. Messages that would have taken weeks to send by mail could now be sent quickly over wires.

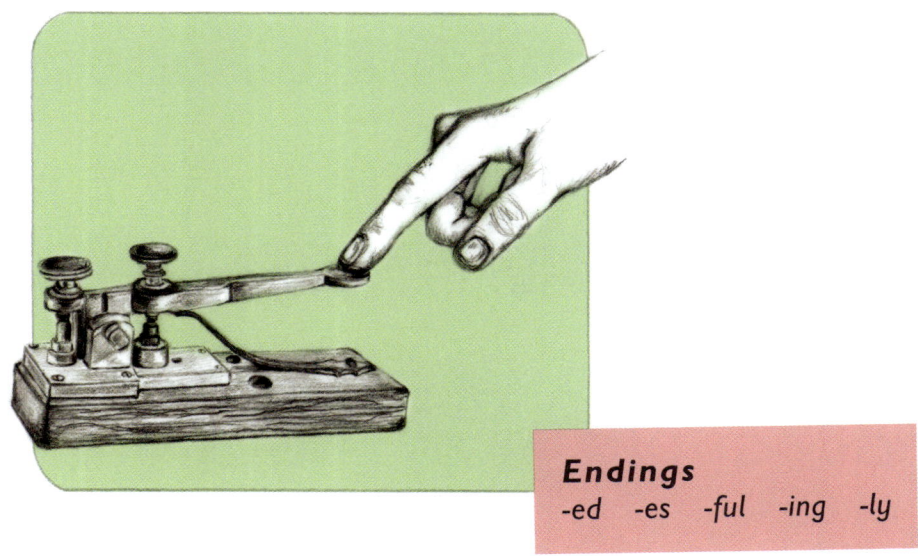

Endings
-ed -es -ful -ing -ly

Section 2: Copywork
Copy and chunk the story.

Samuel Morse loved painting.
S

He painted pictures of famous
H

people. Later in life he tried to
P

find a faster way to send
f

messages. He invented a telegraph.
m

It used Morse code, a system
I

of dots and dashes. Each letter
o

and number had its own code.
a

11D

Section 1: Tricky y Guy, Endings, Silent Letters

1. Read the story to your student.
2. Read it together slowly. Have the student look carefully at each word as you read.
3. Mark **Tricky *y* Guy** in green, **endings** in pink or red, and **silent letters** in orange.

Samuel Morse loved painting. He painted pictures of famous people. Later in life he tried to find a faster way to send messages. He invented a telegraph. It used Morse code, a system of dots and dashes. Each letter and number had its own code. Messages that would have taken weeks to send by mail could now be sent quickly over wires.

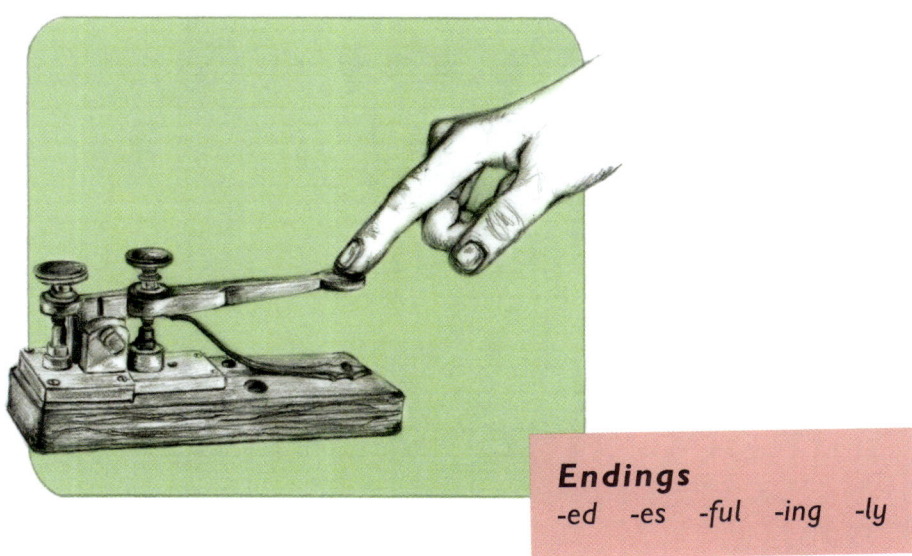

Endings
-ed -es -ful -ing -ly

Section 2: First Dictation

Write this week's story from dictation. Take your time and ask for help if you need it.

Samuel

American Spirit Student 11D

I spelled _____ words correctly.

11E
Section 1: Tricky *y* Guy, Endings, Silent Letters

1. Read the story to your student.
2. Read it together slowly. Have the student look carefully at each word as you read.
3. Mark <u>**Tricky *y* Guy**</u> in green, <u>**endings**</u> in pink or red, and <u>**silent letters**</u> in orange.

Samuel Morse loved painting. He painted pictures of famous people. Later in life he tried to find a faster way to send messages. He invented a telegraph. It used Morse code, a system of dots and dashes. Each letter and number had its own code. Messages that would have taken weeks to send by mail could now be sent quickly over wires.

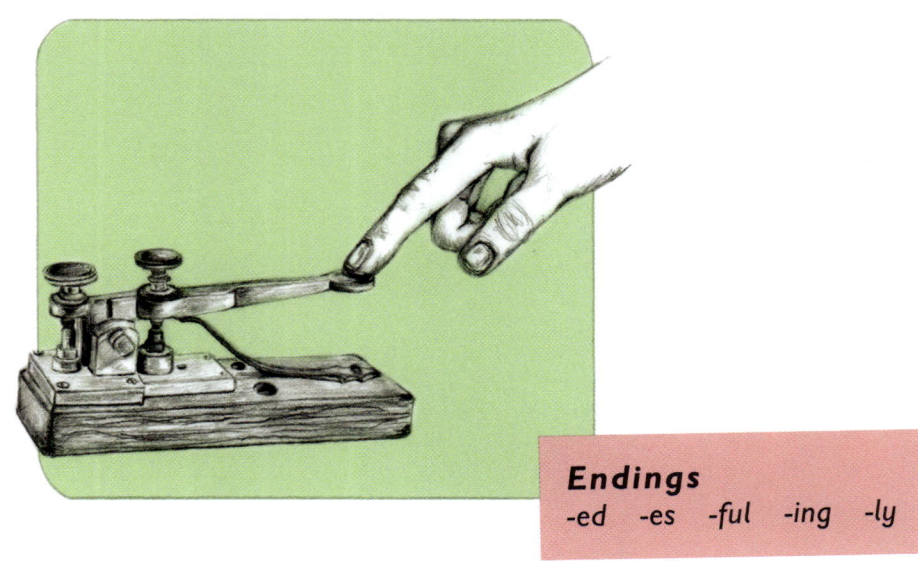

Endings
-ed -es -ful -ing -ly

Section 2: Second Dictation

See if you can write this week's story from dictation without asking for help.

12A Section 1: Tricky y Guy, Endings, Silent Letters

1. Read the story to your student.
2. Read it together slowly. Have the student look carefully at each word as you read.
3. Mark **Tricky *y* Guy** in green, **endings** in pink or red, and **silent letters** in orange.

Twenty thousand men spent six years building a railroad. Some started in Iowa and headed west. Others started in California and worked east. By 1869 the last spike was finally pounded into place. The East and West were linked. After that, many more railroads were built. The railroads joined every part of the country. The folk song "I've Been Working on the Railroad" became very popular.

Endings
-ed -es -ful -ing -ly

American Spirit Student

Section 2: Copywork

Copy and chunk the story.

Twenty thousand men spent six
T
years building a railroad. Some
y
started in Iowa and headed west.
s
Others started in California
O
and worked east. By 1869 the
a
last spike was finally pounded
l
into place. The East and West
i
were linked. After that, many
w
more railroads were built.
m

12B

Section 1: Tricky y Guy, Endings, Silent Letters

1. Read the story to your student.
2. Read it together slowly. Have the student look carefully at each word as you read.
3. Mark **Tricky y Guy** in green, **endings** in pink or red, and **silent letters** in orange.

Twenty thousand men spent six years building a railroad. Some started in Iowa and headed west. Others started in California and worked east. By 1869 the last spike was finally pounded into place. The East and West were linked. After that, many more railroads were built. The railroads joined every part of the country. The folk song "I've Been Working on the Railroad" became very popular.

Endings
-ed -es -ful -ing -ly

Section 2: Copywork

Copy and chunk the story.

By 1869 the last spike was

B

finally pounded into place.

f

The East and West were linked.

T

After that, many more railroads

A

were built. The railroads joined

w

every part of the country. The

e

folk song "I've Been Working on

f

the Railroad" became very popular.

t

American Spirit Student 12B

12C Section 1: Tricky y Guy, Endings, Silent Letters

1. Read the story to your student.
2. Read it together slowly. Have the student look carefully at each word as you read.
3. Mark **Tricky *y* Guy** in green, **endings** in pink or red, and **silent letters** in orange.

Twenty thousand men spent six years building a railroad. Some started in Iowa and headed west. Others started in California and worked east. By 1869 the last spike was finally pounded into place. The East and West were linked. After that, many more railroads were built. The railroads joined every part of the country. The folk song "I've Been Working on the Railroad" became very popular.

Endings
-ed -es -ful -ing -ly

Section 2: Copywork

Copy and chunk the story.

Twenty thousand men spent six

T

years building a railroad. Some

y

started in Iowa and headed west.

s

Others started in California

O

and worked east. By 1869 the

a

last spike was finally pounded

l

into place. The East and West

i

were linked. After that, many

w

more railroads were built.

m

12D

Section 1: Tricky y Guy, Endings, Silent Letters

1. Read the story to your student.
2. Read it together slowly. Have the student look carefully at each word as you read.
3. Mark **Tricky *y* Guy** in green, **endings** in pink or red, and **silent letters** in orange.

Twenty thousand men spent six years building a railroad. Some started in Iowa and headed west. Others started in California and worked east. By 1869 the last spike was finally pounded into place. The East and West were linked. After that, many more railroads were built. The railroads joined every part of the country. The folk song "I've Been Working on the Railroad" became very popular.

Endings
-ed -es -ful -ing -ly

Section 2: First Dictation

Write this week's story from dictation. Take your time and ask for help if you need it.

Twenty

12E Section 1: Tricky y Guy, Endings, Silent Letters

1. Read the story to your student.
2. Read it together slowly. Have the student look carefully at each word as you read.
3. Mark **Tricky y Guy** in green, **endings** in pink or red, and **silent letters** in orange.

Twenty thousand men spent six years building a railroad. Some started in Iowa and headed west. Others started in California and worked east. By 1869 the last spike was finally pounded into place. The East and West were linked. After that, many more railroads were built. The railroads joined every part of the country. The folk song "I've Been Working on the Railroad" became very popular.

Endings
-ed   -es   -ful   -ing   -ly

Section 2: Second Dictation

See if you can write this week's story from dictation without asking for help.

13A

Section 1: All Letter Patterns

1. Read the story to your student.

2. Read it together slowly. Have the student look carefully at each word as you read.

3. This week you and your student will be looking for and marking all six letter patterns that you have learned. They are <u>vowel chunks</u> (yellow), <u>consonant chunks</u> (blue), <u>Bossy *r* chunks</u> (purple), <u>Tricky *y* Guy</u> (green), <u>endings</u> (pink or red), and <u>silent letters</u> (orange).

Would it explode? Would it catch fire? Would it sink? Many people on the dock didn't think the new steamboat would go anywhere. The paddle wheel churned, and smoke puffed. The steamboat began to move steadily up the Hudson River. It cruised along, passing all the other boats as though they were standing still. Robert Fulton and his partner didn't invent the steamboat. They helped to make it practical. Before railroads, rivers were the highways of the country.

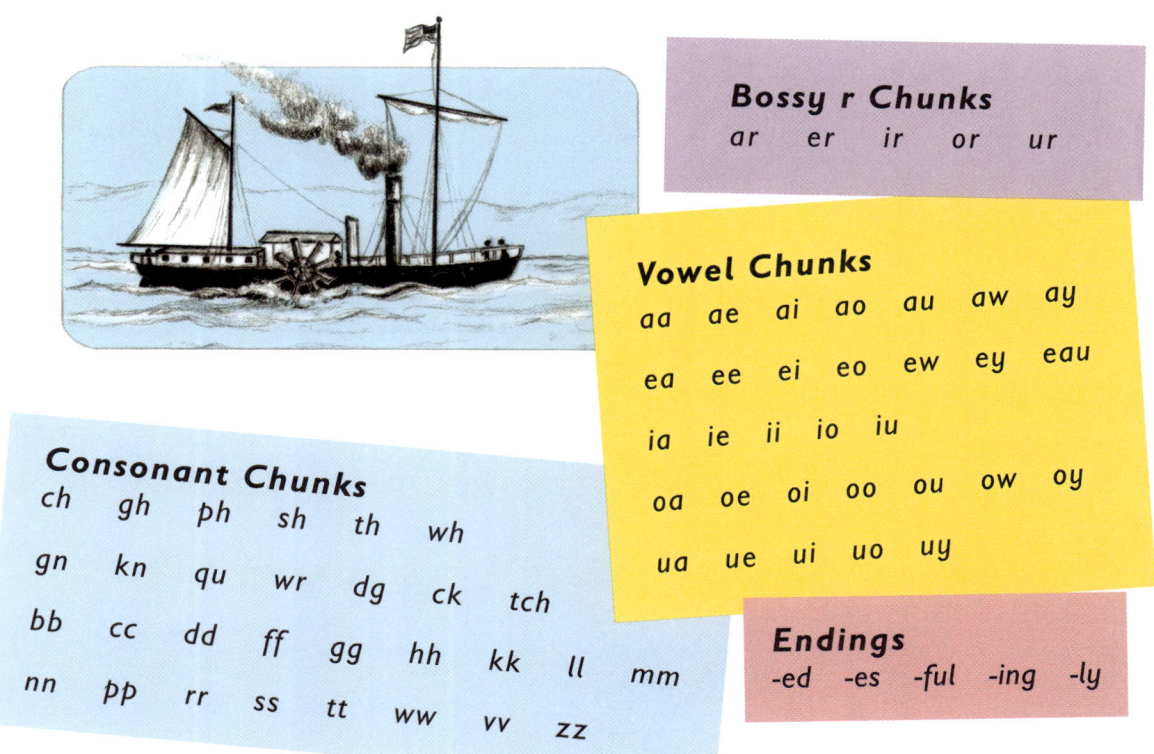

Bossy r Chunks
ar   er   ir   or   ur

Vowel Chunks
aa ae ai ao au aw ay
ea ee ei eo ew ey eau
ia ie ii io iu
oa oe oi oo ou ow oy
ua ue ui uo uy

Consonant Chunks
ch gh ph sh th wh
gn kn qu wr dg ck tch
bb cc dd ff gg hh kk ll mm
nn pp rr ss tt ww vv zz

Endings
-ed -es -ful -ing -ly

124   American Spirit Student

Section 2: Copywork

Copy and chunk the story.

Would it explode? Would it catch
fire? Would it sink? Many people
on the dock didn't think the new
steamboat would go anywhere.
The paddle wheel churned, and
smoke puffed. The steamboat
began to move steadily up the
Hudson River.

13B

Section 1: All Letter Patterns

1. Read the story to your student.
2. Read it together slowly. Have the student look carefully at each word as you read.
3. Together, mark the <u>vowel chunks</u> (yellow), <u>consonant chunks</u> (blue), <u>Bossy *r* chunks</u> (purple), <u>Tricky *y* Guy</u> (green), <u>endings</u> (pink or red), and <u>silent letters</u> (orange).

Would it explode? Would it catch fire? Would it sink? Many people on the dock didn't think the new steamboat would go anywhere. The paddle wheel churned, and smoke puffed. The steamboat began to move steadily up the Hudson River. It cruised along, passing all the other boats as though they were standing still. Robert Fulton and his partner didn't invent the steamboat. They helped to make it practical. Before railroads, rivers were the highways of the country.

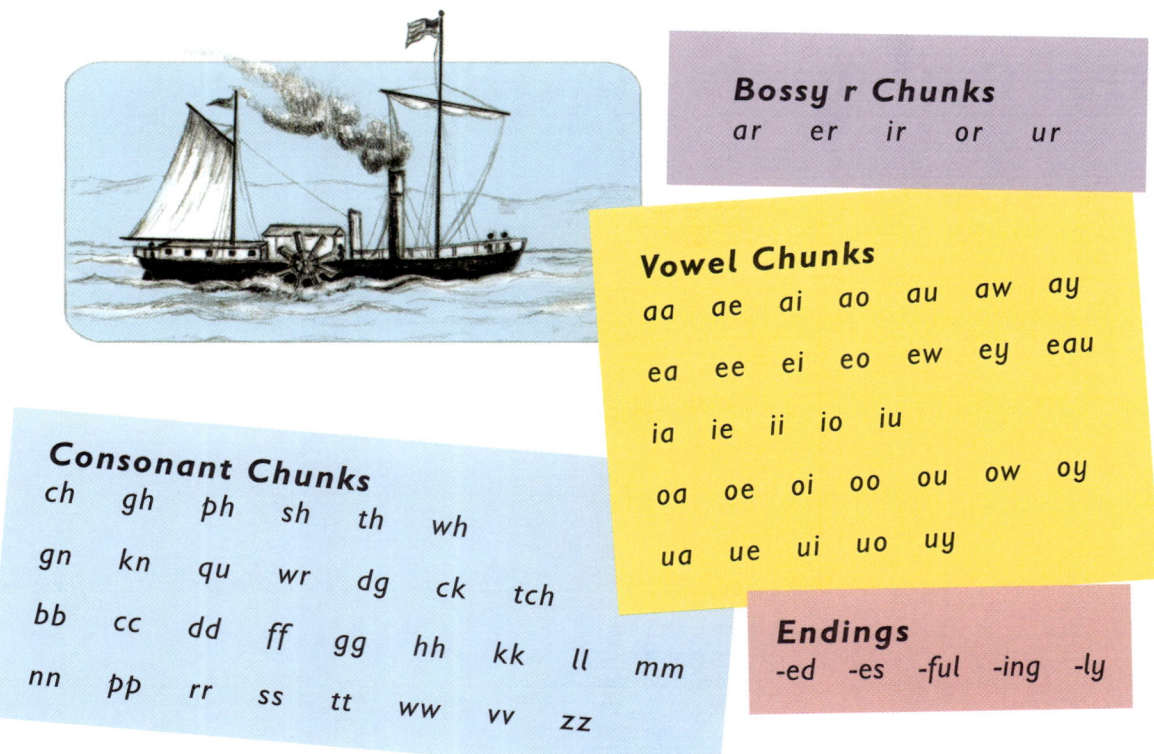

Bossy r Chunks
ar er ir or ur

Vowel Chunks
aa ae ai ao au aw ay
ea ee ei eo ew ey eau
ia ie ii io iu
oa oe oi oo ou ow oy
ua ue ui uo uy

Consonant Chunks
ch gh ph sh th wh
gn kn qu wr dg ck tch
bb cc dd ff gg hh kk ll mm
nn pp rr ss tt ww vv zz

Endings
-ed -es -ful -ing -ly

American Spirit Student

Section 2: Copywork

Copy and chunk the story.

The steamboat began to move
T

steadily up the Hudson River. It
s

cruised along, passing all the other
c

boats as though they were
b

standing still. Robert Fulton and
s

his partner didn't invent the
h

steamboat. They helped to make it
s

practical. Before railroads, rivers
p

were the highways of the country.
w

13C

Section 1: All Letter Patterns

1. Read the story to your student.
2. Read it together slowly. Have the student look carefully at each word as you read.
3. Together, mark the <u>vowel chunks</u> (yellow), <u>consonant chunks</u> (blue), <u>Bossy *r* chunks</u> (purple), <u>Tricky *y* Guy</u> (green), <u>endings</u> (pink or red), and <u>silent letters</u> (orange).

Would it explode? Would it catch fire? Would it sink? Many people on the dock didn't think the new steamboat would go anywhere. The paddle wheel churned, and smoke puffed. The steamboat began to move steadily up the Hudson River. It cruised along, passing all the other boats as though they were standing still. Robert Fulton and his partner didn't invent the steamboat. They helped to make it practical. Before railroads, rivers were the highways of the country.

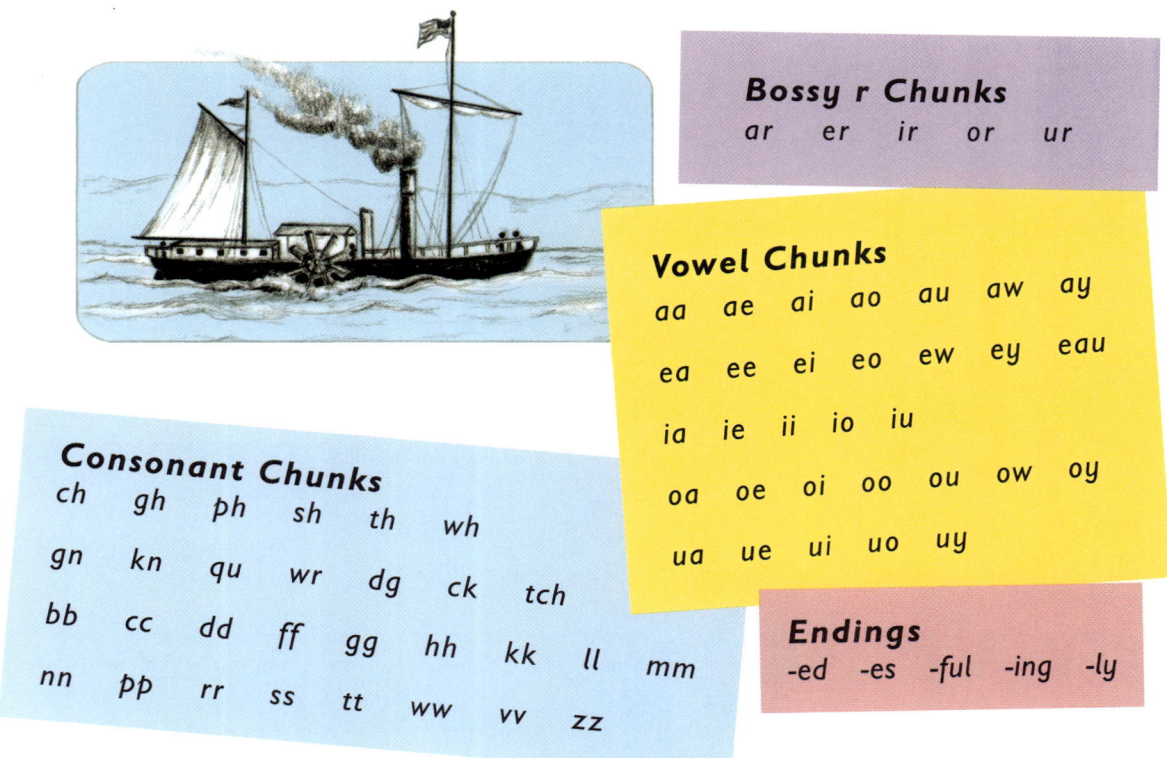

Bossy r Chunks
ar er ir or ur

Vowel Chunks
aa ae ai ao au aw ay
ea ee ei eo ew ey eau
ia ie ii io iu
oa oe oi oo ou ow oy
ua ue ui uo uy

Consonant Chunks
ch gh ph sh th wh
gn kn qu wr dg ck tch
bb cc dd ff gg hh kk ll mm
nn pp rr ss tt ww vv zz

Endings
-ed -es -ful -ing -ly

Section 2: Copywork

Copy and chunk the story.

Would it explode? Would it catch
W
fire? Would it sink? Many people
f
on the dock didn't think the new
o
steamboat would go anywhere.
s
The paddle wheel churned, and
T
smoke puffed. The steamboat
s
began to move steadily up the
b
Hudson River.
H

13D

Section 1: All Letter Patterns

1. Read the story to your student.
2. Read it together slowly. Have the student look carefully at each word as you read.
3. Together, mark the <u>vowel chunks</u> (yellow), <u>consonant chunks</u> (blue), <u>Bossy *r* chunks</u> (purple), <u>Tricky *y* Guy</u> (green), <u>endings</u> (pink or red), and <u>silent letters</u> (orange).

Would it explode? Would it catch fire? Would it sink? Many people on the dock didn't think the new steamboat would go anywhere. The paddle wheel churned, and smoke puffed. The steamboat began to move steadily up the Hudson River. It cruised along, passing all the other boats as though they were standing still. Robert Fulton and his partner didn't invent the steamboat. They helped to make it practical. Before railroads, rivers were the highways of the country.

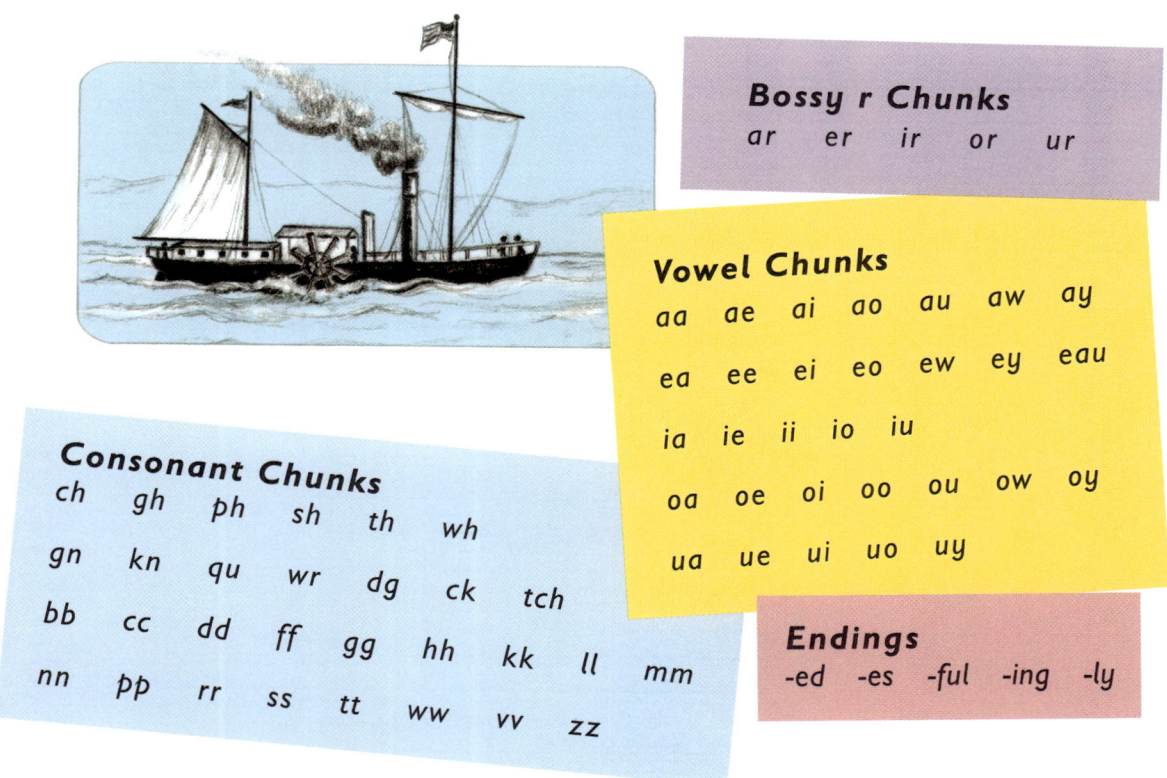

Bossy r Chunks
ar   er   ir   or   ur

Vowel Chunks
aa ae ai ao au aw ay
ea ee ei eo ew ey eau
ia ie ii io iu
oa oe oi oo ou ow oy
ua ue ui uo uy

Consonant Chunks
ch gh ph sh th wh
gn kn qu wr dg ck tch
bb cc dd ff gg hh kk ll mm
nn pp rr ss tt ww vv zz

Endings
-ed -es -ful -ing -ly

American Spirit Student

Section 2: First Dictation

Write this week's story from dictation. Take your time and ask for help if you need it.

Would

13E

Section 1: All Letter Patterns

1. Read the story to your student.
2. Read it together slowly. Have the student look carefully at each word as you read.
3. Together, mark the <u>vowel chunks</u> (yellow), <u>consonant chunks</u> (blue), <u>Bossy *r* chunks</u> (purple), <u>Tricky *y* Guy</u> (green), <u>endings</u> (pink or red), and <u>silent letters</u> (orange).

Would it explode? Would it catch fire? Would it sink? Many people on the dock didn't think the new steamboat would go anywhere. The paddle wheel churned, and smoke puffed. The steamboat began to move steadily up the Hudson River. It cruised along, passing all the other boats as though they were standing still. Robert Fulton and his partner didn't invent the steamboat. They helped to make it practical. Before railroads, rivers were the highways of the country.

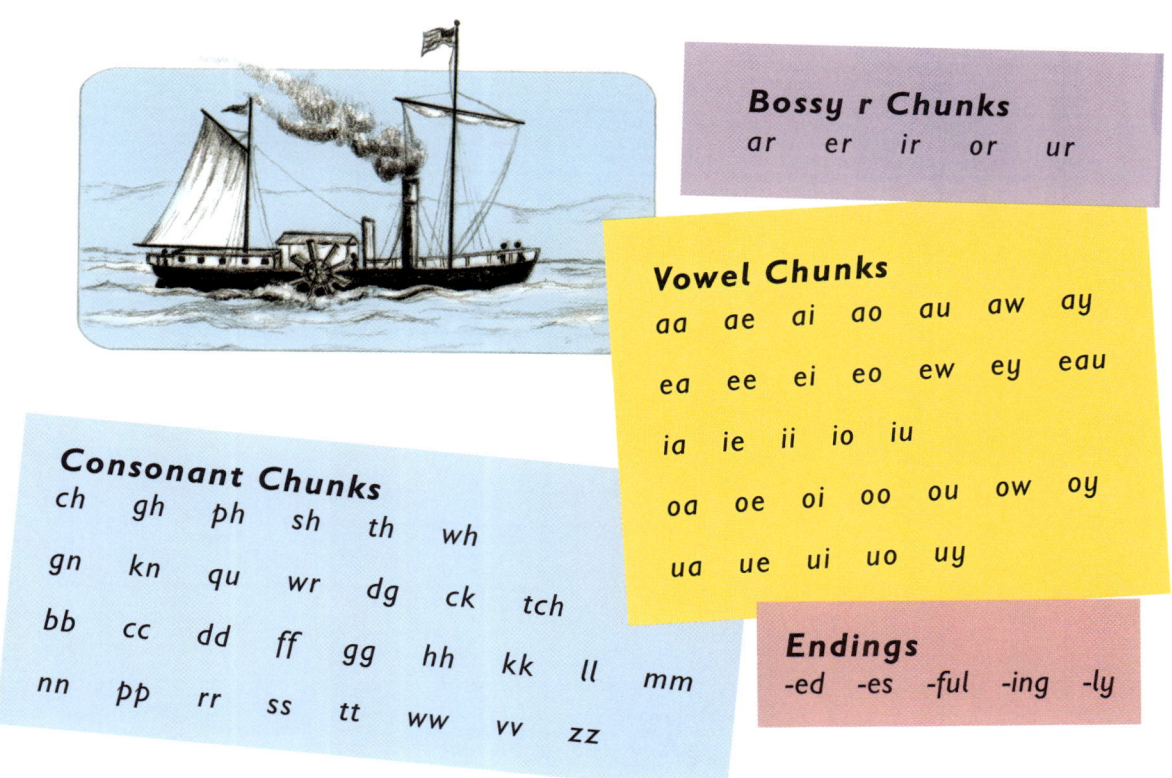

Bossy r Chunks
ar er ir or ur

Vowel Chunks
aa ae ai ao au aw ay
ea ee ei eo ew ey eau
ia ie ii io iu
oa oe oi oo ou ow oy
ua ue ui uo uy

Consonant Chunks
ch gh ph sh th wh
gn kn qu wr dg ck tch
bb cc dd ff gg hh kk ll mm
nn pp rr ss tt ww vv zz

Endings
-ed -es -ful -ing -ly

132 *American Spirit Student*

Section 2: Second Dictation

See if you can write this week's story from dictation without asking for help.

I spelled _____ words correctly.

14A   Section 1: All Letter Patterns

1. Read the story to your student.

2. Read it together slowly. Have the student look carefully at each word as you read.

3. This week you and your student will be looking for and marking all six letter patterns that you have learned. They are **vowel chunks** (yellow), **consonant chunks** (blue), **Bossy r chunks** (purple), **Tricky y Guy** (green), **endings** (pink or red), and **silent letters** (orange).

When it was finished, the Erie Canal linked the Hudson River to Lake Erie. Now there was a safer and cheaper way to get from New York City to the Great Lakes. Some travelers enjoyed the slow, easy pace. They liked the view from the boat's top deck. But people had to listen for the warning, "Low bridge! Everybody down!" Otherwise, they might get knocked overboard!

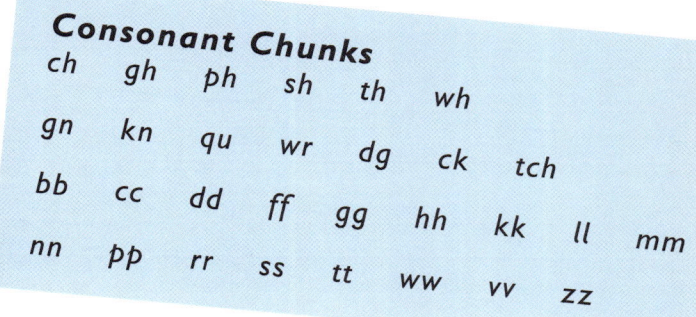

Consonant Chunks
ch   gh   ph   sh   th   wh
gn   kn   qu   wr   dg   ck   tch
bb   cc   dd   ff   gg   hh   kk   ll   mm
nn   pp   rr   ss   tt   ww   vv   zz

Vowel Chunks
aa   ae   ai   ao   au   aw   ay
ea   ee   ei   eo   ew   ey   eau
ia   ie   ii   io   iu
oa   oe   oi   oo   ou   ow   oy
ua   ue   ui   uo   uy

Bossy r Chunks
ar   er   ir   or   ur

Endings
-ed   -es   -ful   -ing   -ly

134   American Spirit Student

Section 2: Copywork
Copy and chunk the story.

When it was finished, the Erie
W

Canal linked the Hudson River to
C

Lake Erie. Now there was a safer
L

and cheaper way to get from
a

New York City to the Great Lakes.
N

Some travelers enjoyed the slow,
S

easy pace. They liked the view
e

from the boat's top deck.
f

14B
Section 1: All Letter Patterns

1. Read the story to your student.
2. Read it together slowly. Have the student look carefully at each word as you read.
3. Together, mark the <u>vowel chunks</u> (yellow), <u>consonant chunks</u> (blue), <u>Bossy *r* chunks</u> (purple), <u>Tricky *y* Guy</u> (green), <u>endings</u> (pink or red), and <u>silent letters</u> (orange).

When it was finished, the Erie Canal linked the Hudson River to Lake Erie. Now there was a safer and cheaper way to get from New York City to the Great Lakes. Some travelers enjoyed the slow, easy pace. They liked the view from the boat's top deck. But people had to listen for the warning, "Low bridge! Everybody down!" Otherwise, they might get knocked overboard!

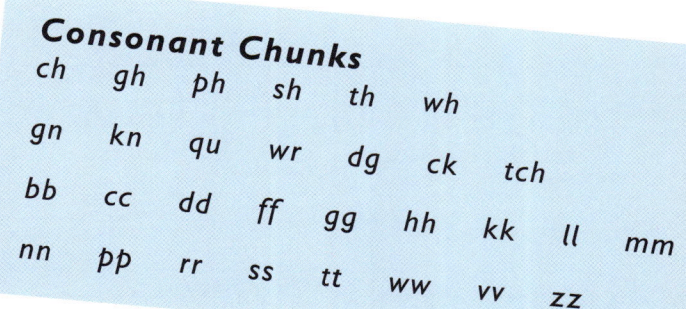

Consonant Chunks
ch gh ph sh th wh
gn kn qu wr dg ck tch
bb cc dd ff gg hh kk ll mm
nn pp rr ss tt ww vv zz

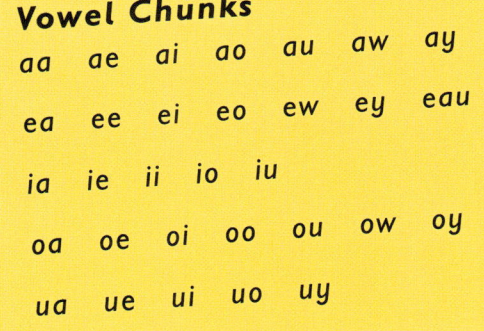

Vowel Chunks
aa ae ai ao au aw ay
ea ee ei eo ew ey eau
ia ie ii io iu
oa oe oi oo ou ow oy
ua ue ui uo uy

Bossy r Chunks
ar er ir or ur

Endings
-ed -es -ful -ing -ly

Section 2: Copywork

Copy and chunk the story.

Now there was a safer way to

get from New York City to the

Great Lakes. Some travelers

enjoyed the slow, easy pace. They

liked the view from the boat's

top deck. But people had to listen

for the warning, "Low bridge!

Everybody down!" Otherwise,

they might get knocked overboard!

American Spirit Student 14B

14C

Section 1: All Letter Patterns

1. Read the story to your student.
2. Read it together slowly. Have the student look carefully at each word as you read.
3. Together, mark the <u>vowel chunks</u> (yellow), <u>consonant chunks</u> (blue), <u>Bossy r chunks</u> (purple), <u>Tricky y Guy</u> (green), <u>endings</u> (pink or red), and <u>silent letters</u> (orange).

When it was finished, the Erie Canal linked the Hudson River to Lake Erie. Now there was a safer and cheaper way to get from New York City to the Great Lakes. Some travelers enjoyed the slow, easy pace. They liked the view from the boat's top deck. But people had to listen for the warning, "Low bridge! Everybody down!" Otherwise, they might get knocked overboard!

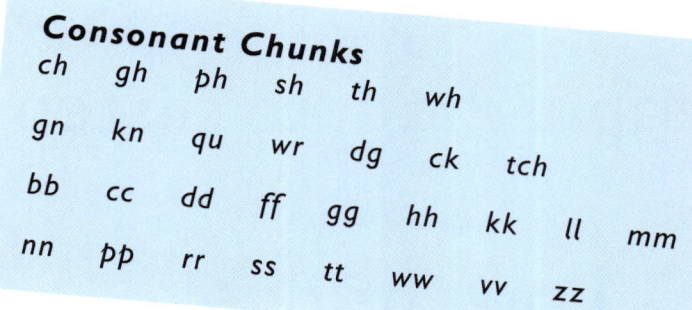

Consonant Chunks

ch gh ph sh th wh
gn kn qu wr dg ck tch
bb cc dd ff gg hh kk ll mm
nn pp rr ss tt ww vv zz

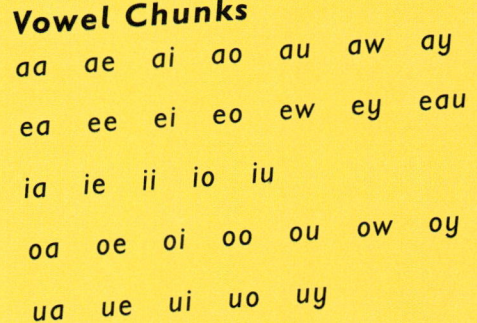

Vowel Chunks

aa ae ai ao au aw ay
ea ee ei eo ew ey eau
ia ie ii io iu
oa oe oi oo ou ow oy
ua ue ui uo uy

Bossy r Chunks

ar er ir or ur

Endings

-ed -es -ful -ing -ly

American Spirit Student

Section 2: Copywork

Copy and chunk the story.

When it was finished, the Erie
W

Canal linked the Hudson River to
C

Lake Erie. Now there was a safer
L

and cheaper way to get from
a

New York City to the Great Lakes.
N

Some travelers enjoyed the slow,
S

easy pace. They liked the view
e

from the boat's top deck.
f

14D

Section 1: All Letter Patterns

1. Read the story to your student.
2. Read it together slowly. Have the student look carefully at each word as you read.
3. Together, mark the <u>vowel chunks</u> (yellow), <u>consonant chunks</u> (blue), <u>Bossy r chunks</u> (purple), <u>Tricky y Guy</u> (green), <u>endings</u> (pink or red), and <u>silent letters</u> (orange).

When it was finished, the Erie Canal linked the Hudson River to Lake Erie. Now there was a safer and cheaper way to get from New York City to the Great Lakes. Some travelers enjoyed the slow, easy pace. They liked the view from the boat's top deck. But people had to listen for the warning, "Low bridge! Everybody down!" Otherwise, they might get knocked overboard!

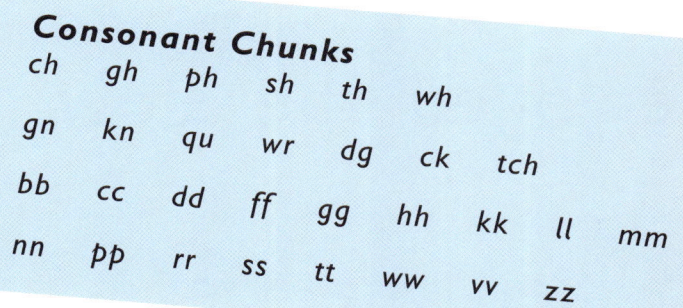

Consonant Chunks

ch gh ph sh th wh
gn kn qu wr dg ck tch
bb cc dd ff gg hh kk ll mm
nn pp rr ss tt ww vv zz

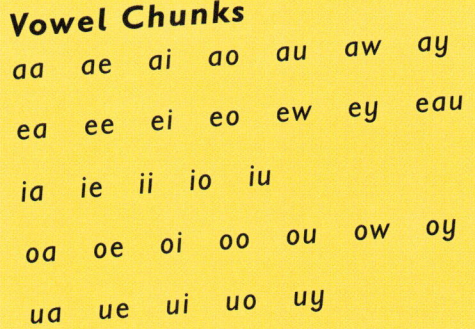

Vowel Chunks

aa ae ai ao au aw ay
ea ee ei eo ew ey eau
ia ie ii io iu
oa oe oi oo ou ow oy
ua ue ui uo uy

Bossy r Chunks

ar er ir or ur

Endings

-ed -es -ful -ing -ly

Section 2: First Dictation

Write this week's story from dictation. Take your time and ask for help if you need it.

When

American Spirit Student 14D   **I spelled _____ words correctly.**

14E

Section 1: All Letter Patterns

1. Read the story to your student.
2. Read it together slowly. Have the student look carefully at each word as you read.
3. Together, mark the **vowel chunks** (yellow), **consonant chunks** (blue), **Bossy r chunks** (purple), **Tricky y Guy** (green), **endings** (pink or red), and **silent letters** (orange).

When it was finished, the Erie Canal linked the Hudson River to Lake Erie. Now there was a safer and cheaper way to get from New York City to the Great Lakes. Some travelers enjoyed the slow, easy pace. They liked the view from the boat's top deck. But people had to listen for the warning, "Low bridge! Everybody down!" Otherwise, they might get knocked overboard!

Consonant Chunks
ch gh ph sh th wh
gn kn qu wr dg ck tch
bb cc dd ff gg hh kk ll mm
nn pp rr ss tt ww vv zz

Vowel Chunks
aa ae ai ao au aw ay
ea ee ei eo ew ey eau
ia ie ii io iu
oa oe oi oo ou ow oy
ua ue ui uo uy

Bossy r Chunks
ar er ir or ur

Endings
-ed -es -ful -ing -ly

142   *American Spirit Student*

Section 2: Second Dictation

See if you can write this week's story from dictation without asking for help.

I spelled _____ words correctly.

15A Section 1: All Letter Patterns

1. Read the story to your student.
2. Read it together slowly. Have the student look carefully at each word as you read.
3. This week you and your student will be looking for and marking all six letter patterns that you have learned. They are **vowel chunks** (yellow), **consonant chunks** (blue), **Bossy r chunks** (purple), **Tricky y Guy** (green), **endings** (pink or red), and **silent letters** (orange).

"Step right up! Step right up! The show is about to begin!" Circuses used to perform in special buildings in big cities. In 1825 one American circus used a large canvas tent for the first time. What a great idea! Now a circus could be held in any city or town. The circus traveled in wagons from place to place. Later, P. T. Barnum began using special train cars to move the circus even farther and faster.

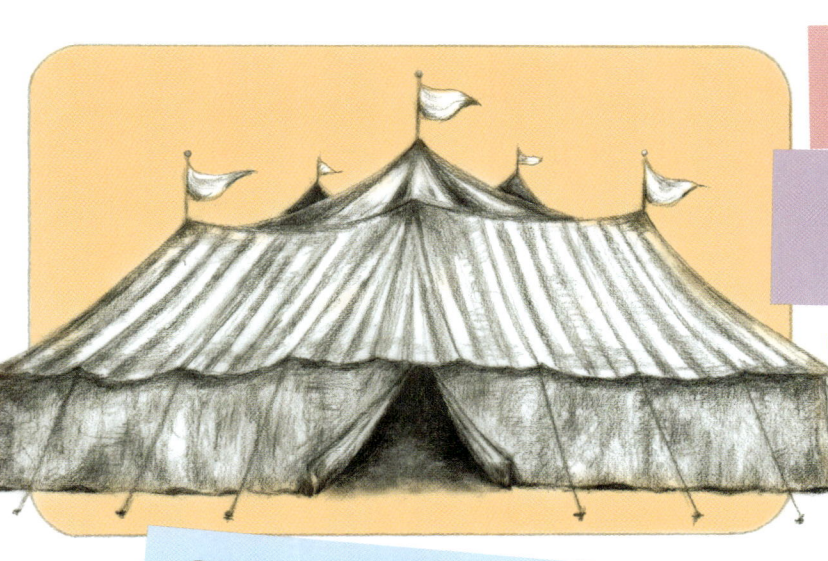

Endings
-ed -es -ful -ing -ly

Bossy r Chunks
ar er ir or ur

Vowel Chunks
aa ae ai ao au aw ay
ea ee ei eo ew ey eau
ia ie ii io iu
oa oe oi oo ou ow oy
ua ue ui uo uy

Consonant Chunks
ch gh ph sh th wh
gn kn qu wr dg ck tch
bb cc dd ff gg hh kk ll mm
nn pp rr ss tt ww vv zz

144 *American Spirit Student*

Section 2: Copywork
Copy and chunk the story.

"Step right up! Step right up!

"S

The show is about to begin!"

T

Circuses used to perform in

C

special buildings in big cities. In

s

1825 one American circus used

1

a large canvas tent for the first

a

time. What a great idea! Now a

t

circus could be held in any city

c

or town.

o

15B

Section 1: All Letter Patterns

1. Read the story to your student.

2. Read it together slowly. Have the student look carefully at each word as you read.

3. Together, mark the **vowel chunks** (yellow), **consonant chunks** (blue), **Bossy r chunks** (purple), **Tricky y Guy** (green), **endings** (pink or red), and **silent letters** (orange).

"Step right up! Step right up! The show is about to begin!" Circuses used to perform in special buildings in big cities. In 1825 one American circus used a large canvas tent for the first time. What a great idea! Now a circus could be held in any city or town. The circus traveled in wagons from place to place. Later, P.T. Barnum began using special train cars to move the circus even farther and faster.

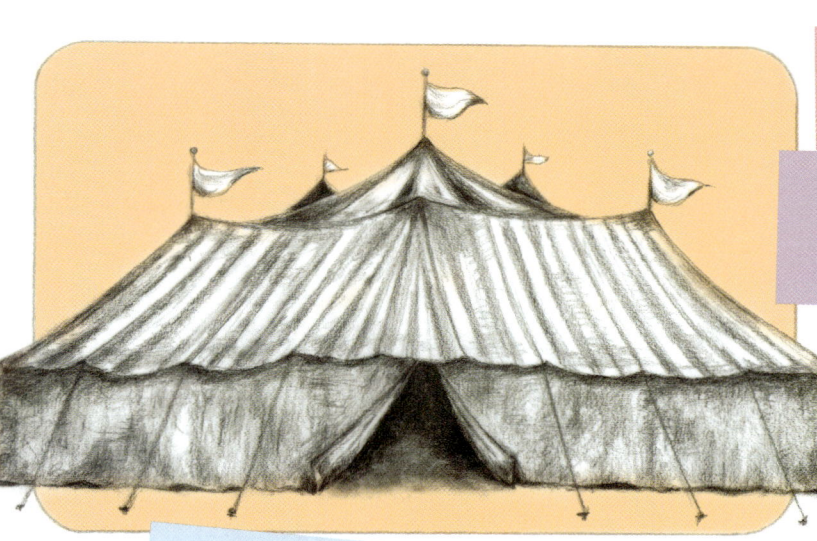

Endings
-ed -es -ful -ing -ly

Bossy r Chunks
ar er ir or ur

Vowel Chunks
aa ae ai ao au aw ay
ea ee ei eo ew ey eau
ia ie ii io iu
oa oe oi oo ou ow oy
ua ue ui uo uy

Consonant Chunks
ch gh ph sh th wh
gn kn qu wr dg ck tch
bb cc dd ff gg hh kk ll mm
nn pp rr ss tt ww vv zz

American Spirit Student

Section 2: Copywork
Copy and chunk the story.

In 1825 one American circus used

a large canvas tent for the first

time. What a great idea! Now a

circus could be held in any city or

town. The circus traveled in

wagons from place to place. Later,

P. T. Barnum began using special

train cars to move the circus even

farther and faster.

American Spirit Student 15B

15C

Section 1: All Letter Patterns

1. Read the story to your student.
2. Read it together slowly. Have the student look carefully at each word as you read.
3. Together, mark the <u>vowel chunks</u> (yellow), <u>consonant chunks</u> (blue), <u>Bossy *r* chunks</u> (purple), <u>Tricky *y* Guy</u> (green), <u>endings</u> (pink or red), and <u>silent letters</u> (orange).

"Step right up! Step right up! The show is about to begin!" Circuses used to perform in special buildings in big cities. In 1825 one American circus used a large canvas tent for the first time. What a great idea! Now a circus could be held in any city or town. The circus traveled in wagons from place to place. Later, P.T. Barnum began using special train cars to move the circus even farther and faster.

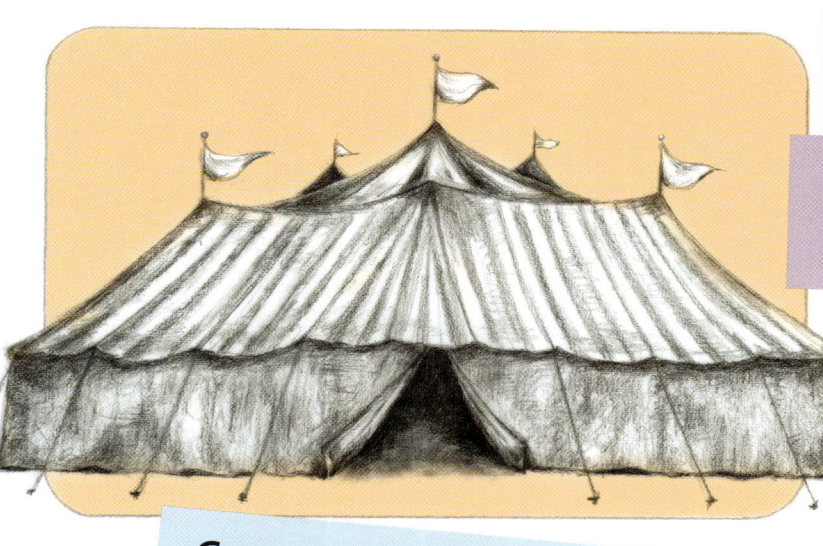

Endings
-ed   -es   -ful   -ing   -ly

Bossy r Chunks
ar   er   ir   or   ur

Vowel Chunks
aa   ae   ai   ao   au   aw   ay
ea   ee   ei   eo   ew   ey   eau
ia   ie   ii   io   iu
oa   oe   oi   oo   ou   ow   oy
ua   ue   ui   uo   uy

Consonant Chunks
ch   gh   ph   sh   th   wh
gn   kn   qu   wr   dg   ck   tch
bb   cc   dd   ff   gg   hh   kk   ll   mm
nn   pp   rr   ss   tt   ww   vv   zz

Section 2: Copywork
Copy and chunk the story.

"Step right up! Step right up!

"S

The show is about to begin!"

T

Circuses used to perform in

C

special buildings in big cities. In

s

1825 one American circus used

1

a large canvas tent for the first

a

time. What a great idea! Now a

t

circus could be held in any city

c

or town.

o

15D

Section 1: All Letter Patterns

1. Read the story to your student.
2. Read it together slowly. Have the student look carefully at each word as you read.
3. Together, mark the <u>**vowel chunks**</u> (yellow), <u>**consonant chunks**</u> (blue), <u>**Bossy r chunks**</u> (purple), <u>**Tricky y Guy**</u> (green), <u>**endings**</u> (pink or red), and <u>**silent letters**</u> (orange).

"Step right up! Step right up! The show is about to begin!" Circuses used to perform in special buildings in big cities. In 1825 one American circus used a large canvas tent for the first time. What a great idea! Now a circus could be held in any city or town. The circus traveled in wagons from place to place. Later, P. T. Barnum began using special train cars to move the circus even farther and faster.

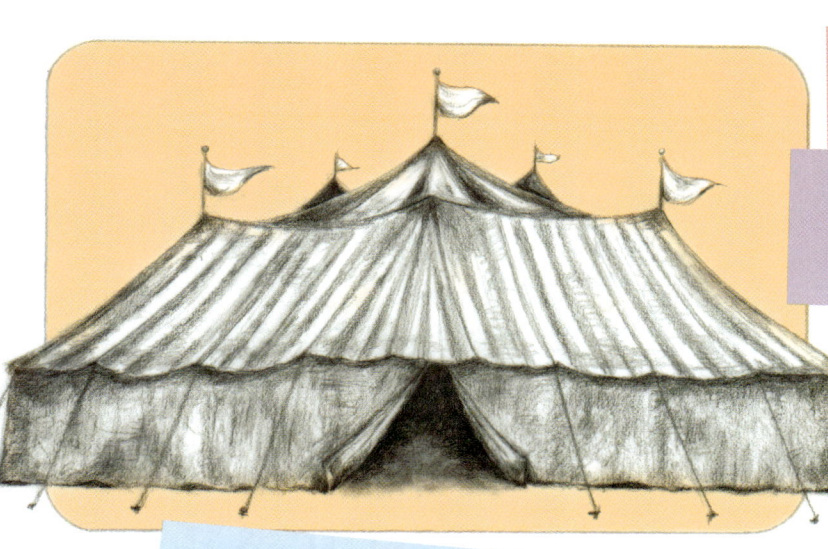

Endings
-ed -es -ful -ing -ly

Bossy r Chunks
ar er ir or ur

Vowel Chunks
aa ae ai ao au aw ay
ea ee ei eo ew ey eau
ia ie ii io iu
oa oe oi oo ou ow oy
ua ue ui uo uy

Consonant Chunks
ch gh ph sh th wh
gn kn qu wr dg ck tch
bb cc dd ff gg hh kk ll mm
nn pp rr ss tt ww vv zz

American Spirit Student

Section 2: First Dictation

Write this week's story from dictation. Take your time and ask for help if you need it.

"Step

I spelled _____ words correctly.

15E

Section 1: All Letter Patterns

1. Read the story to your student.
2. Read it together slowly. Have the student look carefully at each word as you read.
3. Together, mark the <u>vowel chunks</u> (yellow), <u>consonant chunks</u> (blue), <u>Bossy *r* chunks</u> (purple), <u>Tricky *y* Guy</u> (green), <u>endings</u> (pink or red), and <u>silent letters</u> (orange).

"Step right up! Step right up! The show is about to begin!" Circuses used to perform in special buildings in big cities. In 1825 one American circus used a large canvas tent for the first time. What a great idea! Now a circus could be held in any city or town. The circus traveled in wagons from place to place. Later, P. T. Barnum began using special train cars to move the circus even farther and faster.

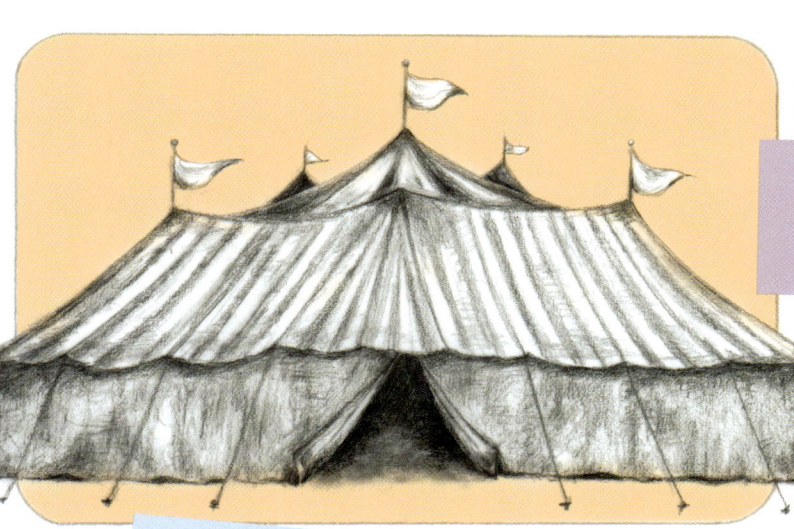

Endings
-ed -es -ful -ing -ly

Bossy r Chunks
ar er ir or ur

Vowel Chunks
aa ae ai ao au aw ay
ea ee ei eo ew ey eau
ia ie ii io iu
oa oe oi oo ou ow oy
ua ue ui uo uy

Consonant Chunks
ch gh ph sh th wh
gn kn qu wr dg ck tch
bb cc dd ff gg hh kk ll mm
nn pp rr ss tt ww vv zz

152 *American Spirit Student*

Section 2: Second Dictation

See if you can write this week's story from dictation without asking for help.

16A

Section 1: All Letter Patterns

1. Read the story to your student.
2. Read it together slowly. Have the student look carefully at each word as you read.
3. This week you and your student will be looking for and marking all six letter patterns that you have learned. They are **vowel chunks** (yellow), **consonant chunks** (blue), **Bossy *r* chunks** (purple), **Tricky *y* Guy** (green), **endings** (pink or red), and **silent letters** (orange).

How could anyone own a person? How could some states allow slavery? Harriet Beecher Stowe believed that slavery was wrong. She knew she had to do something. She wrote stories told from a slave's point of view. The stories became a book called *Uncle Tom's Cabin*. Harriet made the everyday life of slaves real to others. Many people read her book and talked about it. Her writing made a difference.

Consonant Chunks
ch gh ph sh th wh
gn kn qu wr dg ck tch
bb cc dd ff gg hh kk ll mm
nn pp rr ss tt ww vv zz

Vowel Chunks
aa ae ai ao au aw ay
ea ee ei eo ew ey eau
ia ie ii io iu
oa oe oi oo ou ow oy
ua ue ui uo uy

Endings
-ed -es -ful -ing -ly

Bossy r Chunks
ar er ir or ur

American Spirit Student

Section 2: Copywork

Copy and chunk the story.

How could anyone own a person?
H

How could some states allow
H

slavery? Harriet Beecher Stowe
s

believed that slavery was wrong.
b

She knew she had to do
S

something. She wrote stories told
s

from a slave's point of view. The
f

stories became a book called
s

Uncle Tom's Cabin.
U

16B

Section 1: All Letter Patterns

1. Read the story to your student.
2. Read it together slowly. Have the student look carefully at each word as you read.
3. Together, mark the <u>vowel chunks</u> (yellow), <u>consonant chunks</u> (blue), <u>Bossy *r* chunks</u> (purple), <u>Tricky *y* Guy</u> (green), <u>endings</u> (pink or red), and <u>silent letters</u> (orange).

How could anyone own a person? How could some states allow slavery? Harriet Beecher Stowe believed that slavery was wrong. She knew she had to do something. She wrote stories told from a slave's point of view. The stories became a book called *Uncle Tom's Cabin*. Harriet made the everyday life of slaves real to others. Many people read her book and talked about it. Her writing made a difference.

156   *American Spirit Student*

Section 2: Copywork

Copy and chunk the story.

She knew she had to do
something. She wrote stories told
from a slave's point of view. The
stories became a book called
Uncle Tom's Cabin. Harriet made
the everyday life of slaves real
to others. Many people read her
book and talked about it. Her
writing made a difference.

16C

Section 1: All Letter Patterns

1. Read the story to your student.
2. Read it together slowly. Have the student look carefully at each word as you read.
3. Together, mark the **vowel chunks** (yellow), **consonant chunks** (blue), **Bossy r chunks** (purple), **Tricky y Guy** (green), **endings** (pink or red), and **silent letters** (orange).

How could anyone own a person? How could some states allow slavery? Harriet Beecher Stowe believed that slavery was wrong. She knew she had to do something. She wrote stories told from a slave's point of view. The stories became a book called *Uncle Tom's Cabin*. Harriet made the everyday life of slaves real to others. Many people read her book and talked about it. Her writing made a difference.

Consonant Chunks
ch gh ph sh th wh
gn kn qu wr dg ck tch
bb cc dd ff gg hh kk ll mm
nn pp rr ss tt ww vv zz

Vowel Chunks
aa ae ai ao au aw ay
ea ee ei eo ew ey eau
ia ie ii io iu
oa oe oi oo ou ow oy
ua ue ui uo uy

Endings
-ed -es -ful -ing -ly

Bossy r Chunks
ar er ir or ur

American Spirit Student

Section 2: Copywork

Copy and chunk the story.

How could anyone own a person?
H
How could some states allow
H
slavery? Harriet Beecher Stowe
s
believed that slavery was wrong.
b
She knew she had to do
S
something. She wrote stories told
s
from a slave's point of view. The
f
stories became a book called
s
Uncle Tom's Cabin.
U

16D

Section 1: All Letter Patterns

1. Read the story to your student.
2. Read it together slowly. Have the student look carefully at each word as you read.
3. Together, mark the <u>vowel chunks</u> (yellow), <u>consonant chunks</u> (blue), <u>Bossy *r* chunks</u> (purple), <u>Tricky *y* Guy</u> (green), <u>endings</u> (pink or red), and <u>silent letters</u> (orange).

How could anyone own a person? How could some states allow slavery? Harriet Beecher Stowe believed that slavery was wrong. She knew she had to do something. She wrote stories told from a slave's point of view. The stories became a book called *Uncle Tom's Cabin*. Harriet made the everyday life of slaves real to others. Many people read her book and talked about it. Her writing made a difference.

Consonant Chunks
ch gh ph sh th wh
gn kn qu wr dg ck tch
bb cc dd ff gg hh kk ll mm
nn pp rr ss tt ww vv zz

Vowel Chunks
aa ae ai ao au aw ay
ea ee ei eo ew ey eau
ia ie ii io iu
oa oe oi oo ou ow oy
ua ue ui uo uy

Endings
-ed -es -ful -ing -ly

Bossy r Chunks
ar er ir or ur

American Spirit Student

Section 2: First Dictation

Write this week's story from dictation. Take your time and ask for help if you need it.

How

I spelled _____ words correctly.

16E

Section 1: All Letter Patterns

1. Read the story to your student.
2. Read it together slowly. Have the student look carefully at each word as you read.
3. Together, mark the **vowel chunks** (yellow), **consonant chunks** (blue), **Bossy *r* chunks** (purple), **Tricky *y* Guy** (green), **endings** (pink or red), and **silent letters** (orange).

How could anyone own a person? How could some states allow slavery? Harriet Beecher Stowe believed that slavery was wrong. She knew she had to do something. She wrote stories told from a slave's point of view. The stories became a book called *Uncle Tom's Cabin*. Harriet made the everyday life of slaves real to others. Many people read her book and talked about it. Her writing made a difference.

Consonant Chunks
ch gh ph sh th wh
gn kn qu wr dg ck tch
bb cc dd ff gg hh kk ll mm
nn pp rr ss tt ww vv zz

Vowel Chunks
aa ae ai ao au aw ay
ea ee ei eo ew ey eau
ia ie ii io iu
oa oe oi oo ou ow oy
ua ue ui uo uy

Endings
-ed -es -ful -ing -ly

Bossy r Chunks
ar er ir or ur

American Spirit Student

Section 2: Second Dictation

See if you can write this week's story from dictation without asking for help.

I spelled _____ words correctly.

17A

Section 1: All Letter Patterns

1. Read the story to your student.
2. Read it together slowly. Have the student look carefully at each word as you read.
3. Together, mark the vowel chunks, consonant chunks, Bossy *r* chunks, Tricky *y* Guy, endings, and silent letters, using the correct colors for each.

Alexander Graham Bell was interested in hearing and speech. His mother was deaf. His wife was deaf, too. He did experiments. He taught many students how to speak more clearly. He also enjoyed inventing. Aleck built a machine that could send sounds over wires. The telephone changed how people lived. Now they could easily talk to anyone else who had a phone.

Bossy r Chunks
ar er ir or ur

Endings
-ed -es -ful -ing -ly

Vowel Chunks
aa ae ai ao au aw ay
ea ee ei eo ew ey eau
ia ie ii io iu
oa oe oi oo ou ow oy
ua ue ui uo uy

Consonant Chunks
ch gh ph sh th wh
gn kn qu wr dg ck tch
bb cc dd ff gg hh kk ll mm
nn pp rr ss tt ww vv zz

Section 2: Copywork

Copy and chunk the story.

Alexander Graham Bell was
A
interested in hearing and speech.
i
His mother was deaf. His wife
H
was deaf, too. He did experiments.
w
He taught many students how to
H
speak more clearly. He also
s
enjoyed inventing. Aleck built a
e
machine that could send sounds
m
over wires.
o

17B

Section 1: All Letter Patterns

1. Read the story to your student.
2. Read it together slowly. Have the student look carefully at each word as you read.
3. Together, mark the <u>vowel chunks</u>, <u>consonant chunks</u>, <u>Bossy *r* chunks</u>, <u>Tricky *y* Guy</u>, <u>endings</u>, and <u>silent letters</u>, using the correct colors for each.

Alexander Graham Bell was interested in hearing and speech. His mother was deaf. His wife was deaf, too. He did experiments. He taught many students how to speak more clearly. He also enjoyed inventing. Aleck built a machine that could send sounds over wires. The telephone changed how people lived. Now they could easily talk to anyone else who had a phone.

Bossy r Chunks
ar   er   ir   or   ur

Endings
-ed   -es   -ful   -ing   -ly

Vowel Chunks
aa   ae   ai   ao   au   aw   ay
ea   ee   ei   eo   ew   ey   eau
ia   ie   ii   io   iu
oa   oe   oi   oo   ou   ow   oy
ua   ue   ui   uo   uy

Consonant Chunks
ch   gh   ph   sh   th   wh
gn   kn   qu   wr   dg   ck   tch
bb   cc   dd   ff   gg   hh   kk   ll   mm
nn   pp   rr   ss   tt   ww   vv   zz

166   *American Spirit Student*

Section 2: Copywork
Copy and chunk the story.

His wife was deaf, too. He did
H
experiments. He taught many
e
students how to speak more
s
clearly. He also enjoyed inventing.
c
Aleck built a machine that could
A
send sounds over wires. The
s
telephone changed how people
t
lived. Now they could easily talk
l
to anyone else who had a phone.
t

17C

Section 1: All Letter Patterns

1. Read the story to your student.
2. Read it together slowly. Have the student look carefully at each word as you read.
3. Together, mark the vowel chunks, consonant chunks, Bossy r chunks, Tricky y Guy, endings, and silent letters, using the correct colors for each.

Alexander Graham Bell was interested in hearing and speech. His mother was deaf. His wife was deaf, too. He did experiments. He taught many students how to speak more clearly. He also enjoyed inventing. Aleck built a machine that could send sounds over wires. The telephone changed how people lived. Now they could easily talk to anyone else who had a phone.

Bossy r Chunks
ar er ir or ur

Endings
-ed -es -ful -ing -ly

Vowel Chunks
aa ae ai ao au aw ay
ea ee ei eo ew ey eau
ia ie ii io iu
oa oe oi oo ou ow oy
ua ue ui uo uy

Consonant Chunks
ch gh ph sh th wh
gn kn qu wr dg ck tch
bb cc dd ff gg hh kk ll mm
nn pp rr ss tt ww vv zz

168   *American Spirit Student*

Section 2: Copywork

Copy and chunk the story.

Alexander Graham Bell was
A
interested in hearing and speech.
i
His mother was deaf. His wife
H
was deaf, too. He did experiments.
w
He taught many students how to
H
speak more clearly. He also
s
enjoyed inventing. Aleck built a
e
machine that could send sounds
m
over wires.
o

17D

Section 1: All Letter Patterns

1. Read the story to your student.
2. Read it together slowly. Have the student look carefully at each word as you read.
3. Together, mark the <u>vowel chunks</u>, <u>consonant chunks</u>, <u>Bossy *r* chunks</u>, <u>Tricky *y* Guy</u>, <u>endings</u>, and <u>silent letters</u>, using the correct colors for each.

Alexander Graham Bell was interested in hearing and speech. His mother was deaf. His wife was deaf, too. He did experiments. He taught many students how to speak more clearly. He also enjoyed inventing. Aleck built a machine that could send sounds over wires. The telephone changed how people lived. Now they could easily talk to anyone else who had a phone.

Bossy r Chunks
ar   er   ir   or   ur

Endings
-ed   -es   -ful   -ing   -ly

Vowel Chunks
aa ae ai ao au aw ay
ea ee ei eo ew ey eau
ia ie ii io iu
oa oe oi oo ou ow oy
ua ue ui uo uy

Consonant Chunks
ch gh ph sh th wh
gn kn qu wr dg ck tch
bb cc dd ff gg hh kk ll mm
nn pp rr ss tt ww vv zz

Section 2: First Dictation

Write this week's story from dictation. Take your time and ask for help if you need it.

Alexander

I spelled _____ words correctly.

17E

Section 1: All Letter Patterns

1. Read the story to your student.
2. Read it together slowly. Have the student look carefully at each word as you read.
3. Together, mark the **vowel chunks**, **consonant chunks**, **Bossy *r* chunks**, **Tricky *y* Guy**, **endings**, and **silent letters**, using the correct colors for each.

Alexander Graham Bell was interested in hearing and speech. His mother was deaf. His wife was deaf, too. He did experiments. He taught many students how to speak more clearly. He also enjoyed inventing. Aleck built a machine that could send sounds over wires. The telephone changed how people lived. Now they could easily talk to anyone else who had a phone.

Bossy r Chunks
ar   er   ir   or   ur

Endings
-ed   -es   -ful   -ing   -ly

Vowel Chunks
aa ae ai ao au aw ay
ea ee ei eo ew ey eau
ia ie ii io iu
oa oe oi oo ou ow oy
ua ue ui uo uy

Consonant Chunks
ch gh ph sh th wh
gn kn qu wr dg ck tch
bb cc dd ff gg hh kk ll mm
nn pp rr ss tt ww vv zz

172   *American Spirit Student*

Section 2: Second Dictation

See if you can write this week's story from dictation without asking for help.

18A

Section 1: All Letter Patterns

1. Read the story to your student.
2. Read it together slowly. Have the student look carefully at each word as you read.
3. Together, mark the **vowel chunks**, **consonant chunks**, **Bossy *r* chunks**, **Tricky *y* Guy**, **endings**, and **silent letters**, using the correct colors for each.

Tom was always curious. What makes this work? Could it be improved? He tinkered. He learned. Sometimes he failed. But he kept trying and working hard. One of his ideas was an electric light bulb that would keep working for a long time. It was a success! Thomas Edison gathered a group of scientists to work together on new inventions. Today we call this place a research lab. By the time Tom died, his group had over 1,000 patents.

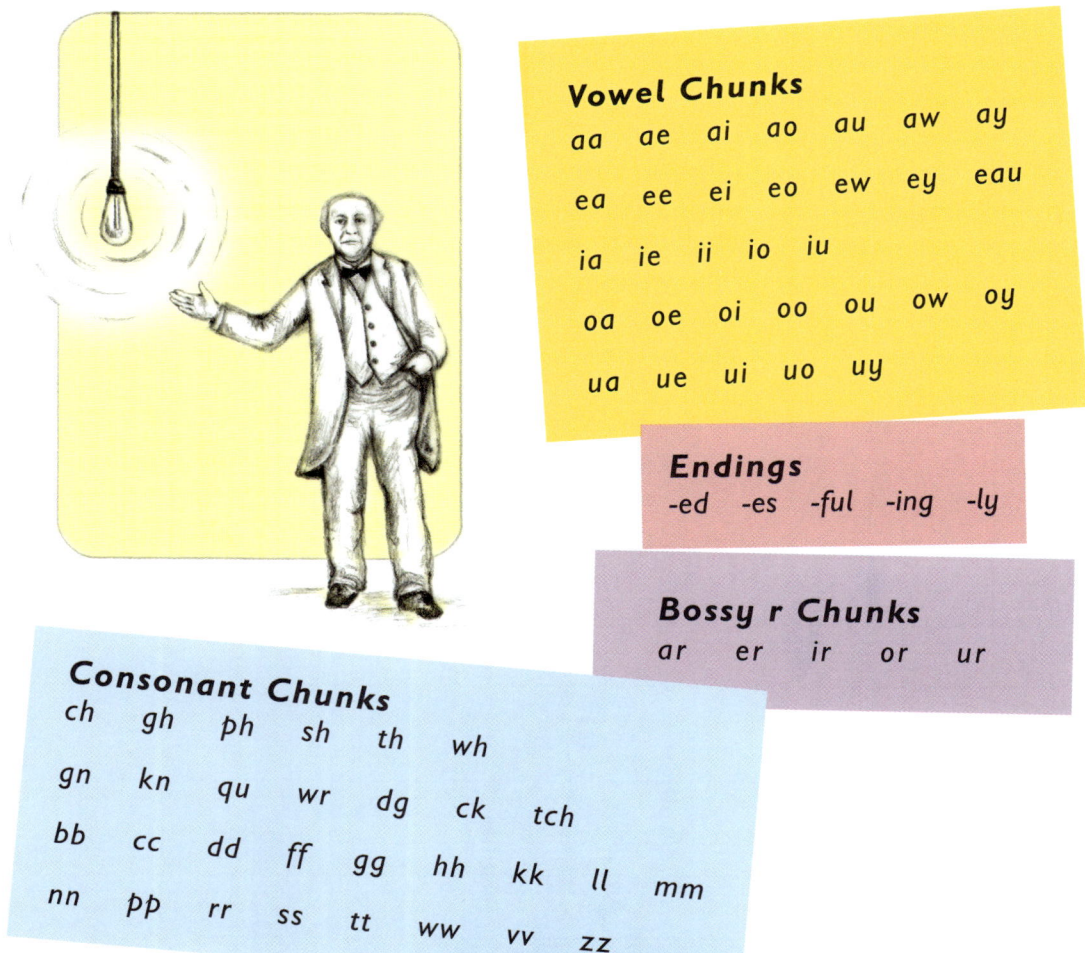

Vowel Chunks
aa ae ai ao au aw ay
ea ee ei eo ew ey eau
ia ie ii io iu
oa oe oi oo ou ow oy
ua ue ui uo uy

Endings
-ed -es -ful -ing -ly

Bossy r Chunks
ar er ir or ur

Consonant Chunks
ch gh ph sh th wh
gn kn qu wr dg ck tch
bb cc dd ff gg hh kk ll mm
nn pp rr ss tt ww vv zz

Section 2: Copywork

Copy and chunk the story.

Tom was always curious. What makes this work? Could it be improved? He tinkered. He learned. Sometimes he failed. But he kept trying and working hard. One of his ideas was an electric light bulb that would keep working for a long time. It was a success!

18B

Section 1: All Letter Patterns

1. Read the story to your student.
2. Read it together slowly. Have the student look carefully at each word as you read.
3. Together, mark the <u>vowel chunks</u>, <u>consonant chunks</u>, <u>Bossy *r* chunks</u>, <u>Tricky *y* Guy</u>, <u>endings</u>, and <u>silent letters</u>, using the correct colors for each.

Tom was always curious. What makes this work? Could it be improved? He tinkered. He learned. Sometimes he failed. But he kept trying and working hard. One of his ideas was an electric light bulb that would keep working for a long time. It was a success! Thomas Edison gathered a group of scientists to work together on new inventions. Today we call this place a research lab. By the time Tom died, his group had over 1,000 patents.

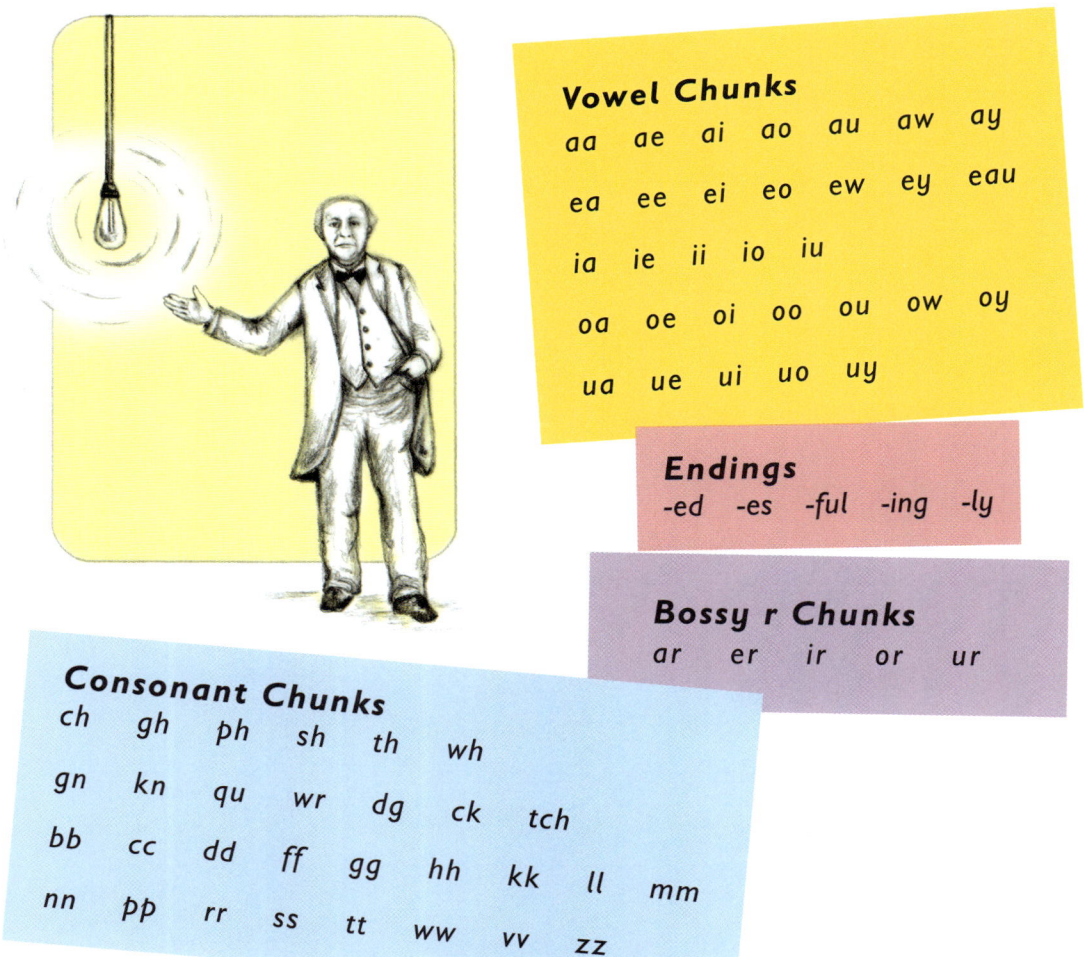

Vowel Chunks

aa ae ai ao au aw ay
ea ee ei eo ew ey eau
ia ie ii io iu
oa oe oi oo ou ow oy
ua ue ui uo uy

Endings

-ed -es -ful -ing -ly

Bossy r Chunks

ar er ir or ur

Consonant Chunks

ch gh ph sh th wh
gn kn qu wr dg ck tch
bb cc dd ff gg hh kk ll mm
nn pp rr ss tt ww vv zz

American Spirit Student

Section 2: Copywork

Copy and chunk the story.

One of his ideas was an electric
O

light bulb that would keep working
l

for a long time. It was a success!
f

Thomas Edison gathered a group
T

of scientists to work together on
o

new inventions. Today we call this
n

place a research lab. By the time
p

Tom died, his group had over
T

1,000 patents.
1

18C

Section 1: All Letter Patterns

1. Read the story to your student.
2. Read it together slowly. Have the student look carefully at each word as you read.
3. Together, mark the <u>vowel chunks</u>, <u>consonant chunks</u>, <u>Bossy *r* chunks</u>, <u>Tricky *y* Guy</u>, <u>endings</u>, and <u>silent letters</u>, using the correct colors for each.

Tom was always curious. What makes this work? Could it be improved? He tinkered. He learned. Sometimes he failed. But he kept trying and working hard. One of his ideas was an electric light bulb that would keep working for a long time. It was a success! Thomas Edison gathered a group of scientists to work together on new inventions. Today we call this place a research lab. By the time Tom died, his group had over 1,000 patents.

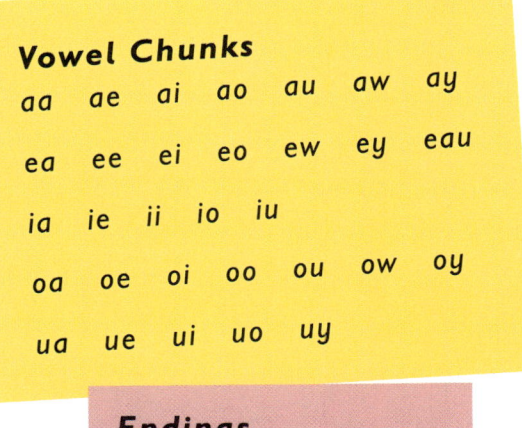

Vowel Chunks

aa ae ai ao au aw ay
ea ee ei eo ew ey eau
ia ie ii io iu
oa oe oi oo ou ow oy
ua ue ui uo uy

Endings
-ed -es -ful -ing -ly

Bossy r Chunks
ar er ir or ur

Consonant Chunks
ch gh ph sh th wh
gn kn qu wr dg ck tch
bb cc dd ff gg hh kk ll mm
nn pp rr ss tt ww vv zz

Section 2: Copywork
Copy and chunk the story.

Tom was always curious. What
T
makes this work? Could it be
m
improved? He tinkered. He learned.
i
Sometimes he failed. But he kept
S
trying and working hard. One of
t
his ideas was an electric light
h
bulb that would keep working for
b
a long time. It was a success!
a

18D

Section 1: All Letter Patterns

1. Read the story to your student.
2. Read it together slowly. Have the student look carefully at each word as you read.
3. Together, mark the <u>vowel chunks</u>, <u>consonant chunks</u>, <u>Bossy *r* chunks</u>, <u>Tricky *y* Guy</u>, <u>endings</u>, and <u>silent letters</u>, using the correct colors for each.

Tom was always curious. What makes this work? Could it be improved? He tinkered. He learned. Sometimes he failed. But he kept trying and working hard. One of his ideas was an electric light bulb that would keep working for a long time. It was a success! Thomas Edison gathered a group of scientists to work together on new inventions. Today we call this place a research lab. By the time Tom died, his group had over 1,000 patents.

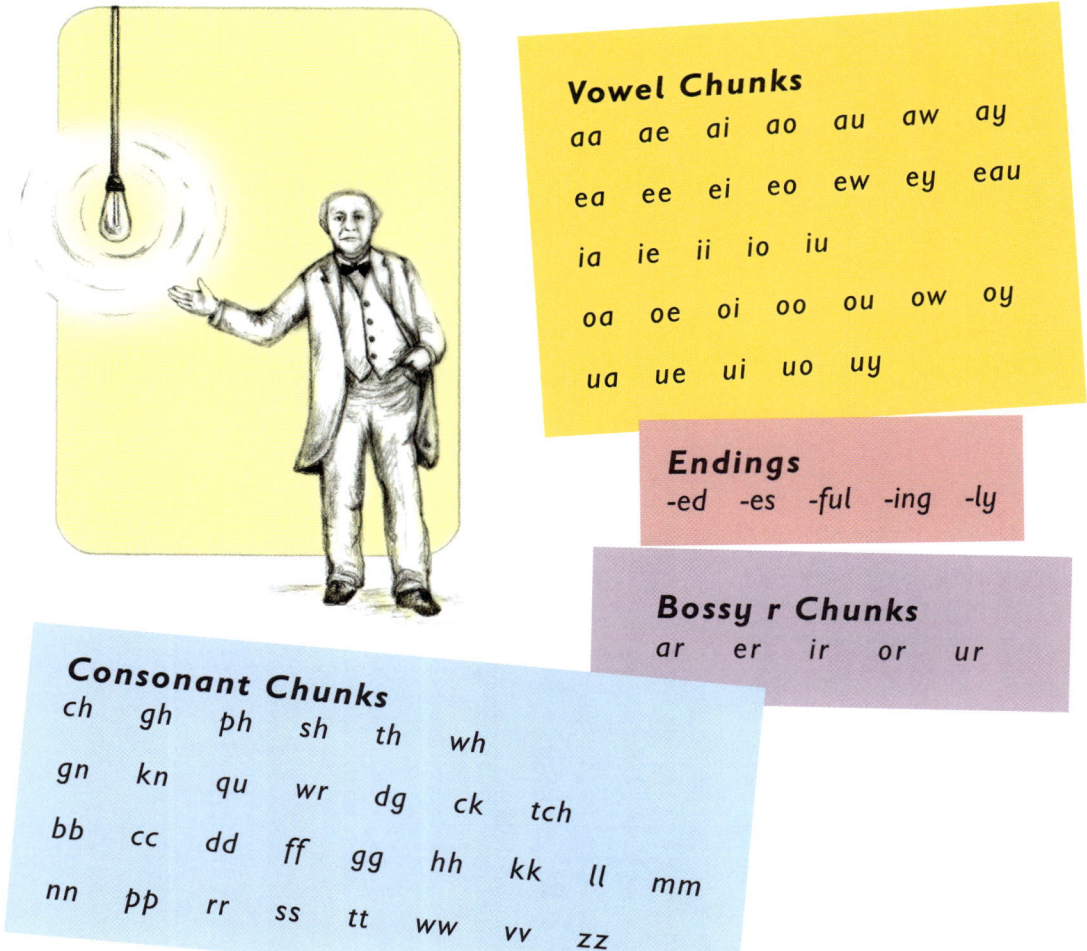

Vowel Chunks

aa ae ai ao au aw ay
ea ee ei eo ew ey eau
ia ie ii io iu
oa oe oi oo ou ow oy
ua ue ui uo uy

Endings
-ed -es -ful -ing -ly

Bossy r Chunks
ar er ir or ur

Consonant Chunks
ch gh ph sh th wh
gn kn qu wr dg ck tch
bb cc dd ff gg hh kk ll mm
nn pp rr ss tt ww vv zz

American Spirit Student

Section 2: First Dictation

Write this week's story from dictation. Take your time and ask for help if you need it.

Tom

I spelled _____ words correctly.

18E

Section 1: All Letter Patterns

1. Read the story to your student.
2. Read it together slowly. Have the student look carefully at each word as you read.
3. Together, mark the <u>vowel chunks</u>, <u>consonant chunks</u>, <u>Bossy *r* chunks</u>, <u>Tricky *y* Guy</u>, <u>endings</u>, and <u>silent letters</u>, using the correct colors for each.

Tom was always curious. What makes this work? Could it be improved? He tinkered. He learned. Sometimes he failed. But he kept trying and working hard. One of his ideas was an electric light bulb that would keep working for a long time. It was a success! Thomas Edison gathered a group of scientists to work together on new inventions. Today we call this place a research lab. By the time Tom died, his group had over 1,000 patents.

Vowel Chunks
aa ae ai ao au aw ay
ea ee ei eo ew ey eau
ia ie ii io iu
oa oe oi oo ou ow oy
ua ue ui uo uy

Endings
-ed -es -ful -ing -ly

Bossy r Chunks
ar er ir or ur

Consonant Chunks
ch gh ph sh th wh
gn kn qu wr dg ck tch
bb cc dd ff gg hh kk ll mm
nn pp rr ss tt ww vv zz

182 *American Spirit Student*

Section 2: Second Dictation

See if you can write this week's story from dictation without asking for help.